UNIQUE
MEETING PLACES IN
GREATER BALTIMORE

To Jim and Caitlin, who found themselves accidental tourists on many of my site visits

UNIQUE MEETING PLACES IN GREATER BALTIMORE

Distinctive Conference and Party Facilities from Downtown to the Eastern Shore

ELISE FORD

EPM
Publications, Inc./McLean, Virginia

Acknowledgments

Thank you to the caterers, event planners, site managers and others who helped me in my research for this book, but most especially to my greatest source of information, my mother, Claire Hartman, who continues to report to me new rental location prospects.

Library of Congress Cataloging-in-Publication Data

Ford, Elise.
    Unique meeting places in Greater Baltimore: distinctive conference and party facilities from downtown to the Eastern Shore
Elise Ford.
      p. cm.
    Includes index.
    ISBN 0-939009-61-7
     1. Convention facilities—Maryland—Baltimore Region—
Guidebooks. I. Title.
TX907.3.M32B354 1992
647—dc20
                           92-6070
                              CIP

EPM Publications, Inc., 1003 Turkey Run Road
   McLean, VA 22101
Printed in the United States of America

Cover and book design by Tom Huestis
Cover drawing by Pauline Lange: George Peabody Library of the
   Johns Hopkins University

Contents

SITES FOR 200 TO 500 PEOPLE

SITES FOR 500 TO 1,000 PEOPLE

SITES FOR MORE THAN 1,000 PEOPLE

How to Use This Book

In conversing with the site managers I met during the research of *Unique Meeting Places in Greater Baltimore*, I often heard the comment, "What a wonderful idea for a book!" Most times I accepted the implied compliment with a modest smile and a thank you. But sometimes I told the truth, which is that the idea for a guide to distinctive conference and party facilities was not wholly my own.

In 1986, a board member of the Greater Washington Society of Association Executives approached me with the proposal that I write such a guide for the Washington area, which I did. The result, *Unique Meeting Places in Greater Washington*, was published in 1988 and is currently in its third edition. The book was tremendous fun to research and write, and I got paid for it. What more could a freelance writer ask for? Another book just like the first, of course.

Riding the coattails of someone else's original thought, I got the brainstorm to author a similar book for some other city. Paris? Well, there was the problem of the commute and then, perhaps, the language. That's when I thought of Baltimore, a journey I could handle by car from my Chevy Chase home, and a parlance well understood by me. Baltimore is where I was born and raised, where my parents, two of my sisters, and my aunt still live. Upon hearing of this book possibility, my mother promptly dispatched to me an envelope full of newspaper and magazine clippings on Baltimore reception sites, and I was on my way.

Like its Washington forerunner, the Baltimore book is intended as an aid for all types of event planners: brides-to-be looking for a wedding site, government officials searching for a historic Baltimore estate at which to entertain visiting dignitaries, charity gala chairs casting about for the perfect, most splendiferous ballroom, corporate meeting planners hunting down a quiet conference center for a business retreat, film studio location experts scouting for a suitable spot to shoot a particular movie scene, moms hoping to find some place other than a pizza joint to throw a child's birthday party, and all other souls frantically in quest of the truly unique event site.

What I hope you'll discover from this guide to Baltimore's uncommon meeting places is that there are so many from which to choose. For a sense of history, try staging an intimate soiree around the same dining room table where H.L. Mencken and his cronies sat drinking and exchanging witticisms (at the H.L. Mencken House), or else celebrate in a modern building saluting Maryland's heritage (the Maryland Historical Society). For a hint of whimsey, carry a crowd to the Studio at Art and Architectural Design, a century-old parsonage that meshes stained-glass and Gothic windows with playful color schemes and offbeat furnishings. For just plain fun, host a bay-sailing party aboard the *Lady Baltimore*, or a stationary sightseeing extravaganza from a top floor of one of the Inner Harbor's skyscrapers: the World Trade Center or the Glass View in the Bank Center Building. All of these places, and many more, are available to you and are included in *Unique Meeting Places in Greater Baltimore*.

If you know exactly where you want to stage your Baltimore event, simply flip to the Alphabetic Index and find the page number for the site description. Each of the guide's nearly 90 entries provides facts about capacity, location, food and beverage arrangements, rates, limitations and restrictions, lead time for reserving, and facilities for the physically handicapped.

If you haven't made up your mind about a site or are just starting your search, this guide should help you pinpoint the one place that meets all your criteria. In addition, the book may be used, first, as a tool in the meeting planning process to help you arrive at answers to basic questions, the same questions you can expect to be asked by the staff at each site. These questions are:

- When is the event taking place?
- How many people will be attending?
- What type of event will it be?
- Do you want it indoors, outdoors or both?
- What is your budget?
- What are your special requirements? For example, do you have specific music, food or drink, or equipment requirements? Do you want dancing?
- Do you want everyone in one room or do you care whether your group gets split?

The guide is organized by capacity categories since the one piece of information that meeting planners and hosts often know from the start is the general number of people expected to attend the function. Please note: The sites included in each section are those whose maximum capacities fall into a particular category. Maximum capacities reflect the total space available, usually including the grounds. Consider the example of Oregon Ridge Lodge and Park: this site falls into the category of "Sites for More Than 1,000 People" since the park grounds can accommodate thousands of partyers; the lodge by itself, however, can fit up to 600, max.

If you wish to know how many people can be accommodated indoors alone or within one portion of the site, or for a particular type of event, you should refer to the specific information provided for each site.

Once you've determined the exact sites that can hold your group, it's up to you to choose the place you want. A Topical Cross-reference at the back of the book identifies sites by special interest. If you're keen on throwing a large outdoor party, look under the "Parks and Pavilions" heading and you'll find several choices, Quiet Waters Park in Annapolis and the Baltimore Zoo in midtown Baltimore, among them. If you're holding an overnight business event, go down the list of the overnight conference centers. Should you opt for an art-full setting, you'll want to consider the "Museums" listings, all 19 of them.

Perhaps you're not interested in traveling far; in such case, you should refer to the Geographic Index for sites located near your home or office, or near your group's central headquarters. Certainly the budget factor will figure in your choice of a site. Specific rates are provided in each site description (unless a location declined to include them), so simply consult there to decide whether your budget covers the stated costs. The rates quoted herein are those provided by the sites in late 1991.

In addition to rental costs, there are usually other expenses, some of which can be quite substantial. Take catering, for instance. A three-hour cocktail reception for 50 people is likely to run you about $2,000; adding dinner can at least double that; and if you really want to go down in history, some caterers will gladly help you spend as much as $250 per person. Tent rental is another major expense.

11

Prices start in the hundreds-of-dollars range for a small tent and go as high as the tens of thousands of dollars for the largest size tent equipped with special, but sometimes necessary, items such as lighting, guttering, a dance floor, and heaters.

You should also read carefully the "Limitations and Restrictions" information provided for each site. These conditions on the use of a site let you know whether, in fact, you are eligible to rent the site. Some locations are quite exclusive: The Engineering Center requires not only that you be a member of its club, but that your membership be at least a year old for you to qualify to reserve the mansion for a special event. Other locations, like the Aspen Institute's Wye Center, allow only corporate or organization users, no individuals.

The "Limitations and Restrictions" guidelines also delineate the general rules of usage to which meeting places ask you to adhere when you rent their facilities. One site may prohibit smoking, for example, and another not allow dancing. These meeting places are special spaces, after all, and site managers are simply trying to protect their facilities from the inevitable wear and tear that partygoers can unleash upon the surroundings. Certain locations that you might expect to find in this guidebook, for example, the Edgar Allan Poe House, are absent for the very reason that special events in the past caused too much damage, leaving these sites no longer rentable. So be sure to pay attention to the use guidelines and treat a site accordingly.

There are other things you should be aware of as you read this book. The word "reception" used throughout refers to any standup event; the word "banquet" refers to any type of sit-down function. The serving of alcohol is permitted at most sites; therefore, the book notes only exceptions or restrictions on the use thereof. For example, both Quiet Waters Park and Downs Memorial Park in Annapolis allow only keg beer, and no wine or hard liquor.

You'll notice the recurring phrase "Call for availability" when you come to the "Lead Time for Reservations" portion of the page. While many places are fairly specific about their reservation schedules, others find their schedules less predictable. These facilities prefer to have you give them a call, no matter the lead time, on the chance that a cancellation or other unexpected circumstance makes their site available when you need it.

The question "Facilities for the Physically Handicapped?" appears at the end of each entry. A check mark under "Yes" indicates that the site itself and a restroom are accessible to someone in a wheelchair. A check mark under "No" means that neither the site nor its restrooms are easily accessible to someone in a wheelchair. A "Some" notation followed by a brief explanation lets you know that the site is partially accessible to a person in a wheelchair and just what those accessible facilities are. All sites recommend that you call ahead to notify staff when your party includes handicapped individuals so that you find out the full details of accessibility and to ensure that the staff makes the proper plans.

In all, the book offers you 89 unique meeting places from which to choose. I hope my descriptions make it easy for you to decide the site best suited to your group and occasion. As for how to make your event memorable—that part's up to you: good luck!

Maryvale Castle, Brooklandville

Sites for
Fewer than 100 People

THE ASPEN INSTITUTE'S WYE CENTER

Carmichael Road
Mailing address: P.O. Box 222
Queenstown, Maryland 21658
410/827-7168

A conference center treasure on the Eastern Shore

The Aspen Institute is an international, nonprofit organization started in 1950 with the aim of designing programs to enhance leadership qualities and provoke stimulating discussion of the issues of the day among leaders gathered from many segments of society: government, academia, business, the nonprofit sector, the media, and so on. The Institute's Wye Center opened in 1978 as a place to host its own seminars as well as those of outside groups whose goals are compatible with Aspen's.

The Aspen Institute's Wye Center operates three extraordinary and distinctly different conference facilities, each located at a distance from one another on 1,000 or so acres of pristine Eastern Shore countryside fronting the Wye River. The River House is a brick country mansion that is both homey and elegant. Guests stay in one of 25 luxuriously appointed bedrooms in the River House itself or in the River House Inn and Cottage located across the terraced courtyard. The many-sided conference room on the lower level has a custom-made, many-sided conference table and rolling, full-cushioned chairs. Other spaces include an exercise room, break-out room, den-like game room, wicker-furnished sun room, an inviting drawing room, and pleasing green and floral-adorned dining room.

The Houghton House is a Georgian-style manor, a trifle more formal than River House. There are 22 individually decorated bedrooms, a conference room with another custom-made table and a comfortable sitting area off to one side, and a paneled library used as an auxiliary meeting space. When you're ready to relax, you can sit on the wide, rounded bay-window seat of the marvelous yellow-toned drawing room and stare out to the river, stroll the 200-year-old terraced gardens, work out in the exercise room, or retire to one of the second floor's cozy sitting rooms.

Wye Woods is the third offering, a complex of rustic, cedar-shingled lodges and buildings on the banks of the Wye River. Camp-casual in atmosphere, Wye Woods' meeting rooms are in a barn-like structure, its dining room in a river-facing pavilion.

You can reserve the entire Wye Center for a retreat or just one of its three facilities. Whatever your choice, you receive a complete range of conference services and equipment, as well as on-site and off-site recreation opportunities.

CAPACITY

Conference: 82 using all three facilities
Overnight accommodations: 82

LOCATION

From the Bay Bridge, travel on Rt. 50 east for 12 miles. Turn right a half mile after milepost 49, at Carmichael Road. You'll see a sign marked "Aspen/Wye Institutes." Proceed about four miles to the center.

FOOD/BEVERAGE

The Marriott Corporation handles all the catering at this site. Each facility has its own kitchen.

LIMITATIONS/RESTRICTIONS

Use of the Wye Center is restricted to adult groups, specifically businesses, nonprofit agencies, education organizations, and others who wish to hold a conference or training session. The center is not available for social events unaffiliated with a scheduled conference. Although the center is primarily an overnight facility, it does allow nonresidential day meetings, when space and schedule permit. Smoking is permitted outside only at each location.

LEAD TIME FOR RESERVATIONS

Call about six to nine months ahead to book your conference.

RATES

Call for rates.

FACILITIES FOR THE PHYSICALLY HANDICAPPED?
YES NO SOME
X

BALTIMORE STREETCAR MUSEUM

1901 Falls Road

Baltimore, Maryland 21211

Mailing Address: P.O. Box 4881

Baltimore, Maryland 21211

410/547-0264

A nostalgic ride back in time

If you grew up in Baltimore before 1963 you might remember streetcars, those clanging trolleys that rode on rails throughout the city. Should memory fail or if you are too young to know the pleasure of an excursion aboard a streetcar, you'll want to get yourself down to the Baltimore Streetcar Museum. Better yet, invite your friends and make a party of it. The museum is a favorite spot for children's celebrations, as well as for political fundraisers, retirement galas, and other adult socials.

You use the visitors center for your food and beverage setups. This building, designed to resemble the streetcar terminals of old, is pretty utilitarian inside. The main exhibit room feels and looks like a classroom, thanks to its white tile floor and white cement-block walls. Exhibits display model trolley cars and trace the history of the streetcar era, from 1859 to 1963. A film entitled *Rails into Yesterday* reveals the role streetcars played in Baltimore's development. Outside the museum are a wide loop of lawn and the carhouse, which you are welcome to explore. The carhouse contains more than 12 vehicles representing different versions of streetcars. The greatest thrill of holding a party here is, of course, the ride aboard the streetcar. It's funny how the (relatively) slow motion of the car, the authentic dress of the conductor, and the trolley's old-fashioned interior really work to re-create a sense of times gone by. Private parties are entitled to unlimited rides!

CAPACITY

Reception: 100 or so inside, hundreds when you use the outside
Banquet: about 40 to 50 inside, about 100 outside

LOCATION

The museum is located in downtown Baltimore, under the
North Avenue Bridge, three blocks from Pennsylvania Station.

FOOD/BEVERAGE

There is no kitchen facility. You make all the catering
arrangements yourself, including obtaining the tables and
chairs.

LIMITATIONS/RESTRICTIONS

The museum is available for parties anytime during the week,
Saturday during the day November through May, Saturday and
Sunday evenings, year-round. Smoking is prohibited inside the
museum and on the trolleys. Music and dancing are allowed but
are best kept outside, given the size limitations of the visitors
center.

LEAD TIME FOR RESERVATIONS

Call four weeks in advance.

RATES

For parties of under 50 people, $100 an hour; for parties of 50
to 99 people, $150 an hour; for parties of 100 to 299 people,
$300 an hour. A two-hour minimum is required for parties of
up to 299 people. For parties of 300 or more people, $500 an
hour, with a three-hour minimum.
Children's parties for kids under 12, $50 an hour, with a two-
hour minimum, and limited to 25 children. The site requires
that you have one adult attending for every six kids.

FACILITIES FOR THE PHYSICALLY HANDICAPPED?
YES NO SOME
     X

The visitors center is handicapped accessible, but the streetcars
really are not.

BELMONT CONFERENCE CENTER

6555 Belmont Woods Road
Elkridge, Maryland 21227
410/796-4300
FAX: 410/796-4565

Historic Georgian manor house and hundreds of wooded acres

Belmont's history begins in 1738, when the mansion was built, and is full of the stuff of novels: the making of a family fortune, the gambling away of the fortune by a dissolute descendant, murder of one family member by a mad cousin, ghosts, romance, and revolution. Things are a little quieter around the 82-acre estate now. Belmont is an elegant overnight conference center, and its vast acreage of lush fields, gardens, and woods makes it a spectacular place for a business retreat.

You may use one or all three conference facilities on the property: the Manor House, the Stable, and Dobbin House. The Manor House holds 16 bedrooms that can accommodate 26 guests, a modern conference room, a dining room, a drawing room, a library, a tea room, and a ballroom, each graciously appointed. A shaded brick patio adjoining the back of the house gives you a view of the pool, tennis court, fitness trail, and woods rolling back towards the unseen Patapsco River.

The Stable, though thoroughly modern inside, was originally the old stable and garage for the estate owners. This is the building you use for nonresidential day meetings.

Dobbin House is situated in its own secluded paradise, not too far from the Manor House. You can hold a small overnight conference here using the house's five private bedrooms, living room and dining room, or you can supplement Manor House bedroom accommodations by using Dobbin House solely for its five guest rooms.

20

CAPACITY

Reception: 35
Banquet: 35
Garden party: 100 to 150
Meeting: 35
Overnight accommodations: 31. Belmont can arrange for additional, nearby sleeping accommodations when the number of your party exceeds 31.

LOCATION

Head south on I-95 to the Route 100 exit and go in the direction of Glen Burnie. Travel a short distance on Rt. 100 until you reach Rt. 1, where you'll turn left. Follow Rt. 1 to Montgomery Road and turn left. From Montgomery Road, turn right on Elibank Drive and then take your immediate left onto Belmont Woods Road. Follow the signs to Belmont.

FOOD/BEVERAGE

Belmont caters all conference meals and works with the group to plan the menus.

LIMITATIONS/RESTRICTIONS

No specific limitations; discuss your requirements with management.

LEAD TIME FOR RESERVATIONS

At least eight weeks, but Belmont will accept reservations two years in advance.

RATES

Manor House: $2,400 per night.
Dobbin House: $450 per night.
Meals: $65 per person per day (covers the costs of three meals and two coffee breaks).
Stable: $500 per day, with a $25 per-person food service charge.

FACILITIES FOR THE PHYSICALLY HANDICAPPED?
YES NO SOME
X

The Stable and Dobbin House are handicapped accessible, but not the Manor House.

DONALDSON BROWN CENTER

200 Mt. Ararat Farm Road
Port Deposit, Maryland 21904
800/468-4761
FAX: 410/378-4892

Georgian estate overlooking the Susquehanna River

You know, the Susquehanna River is not that far away from Baltimore, or from Wilmington, Philadelphia, or Washington, D.C. That's what Dupont executive F. Donaldson Brown realized in 1935 when he scooped up 24 acres of prime promontory planted above the Susquehanna River and built himself a handsome Georgian-style mansion. A native of Maryland (though a graduate of a Virginia college), Brown left his estate to the University of Maryland who, since 1965, has run the place as a private conference center. The center is available primarily to business and educational groups for day meetings and overnight conferences, but it will consider requests from other kinds of organizations for other functions.

The mansion holds 10 main rooms on its first floor and 12 bedrooms that can sleep 30 guests on its second floor. Down the driveway is a carriage house, once a stable, that can sleep 22 people in nine dormitory-like rooms. Donaldson Brown was a wealthy man (this was just one of his six homes), and it shows. Mansion rooms are spacious with high ceilings, lots of hand-carved mahogany woodwork, and many of the original furnishings. There's a modern conference space, a really wonderful living room to get acquainted in (leather loveseats in front of a working fireplace are one highlight), a billiards room, a den, a breakfast room, and a dining room with multiple long windows looking out on the back lawn and the Susquehanna. The second floor of the carriage house offers a more casual spot for mingling and meeting.

Your events can take place outdoors, too, on the well-tended and wide back lawn, where you have the most breathtaking view of the river. Tennis and hiking are your best bets for outdoor recreation.

CAPACITY

Meeting: 40, classroom style; 65, theater-style
Overnight accommodations: 30 in the mansion (sharing 12 bedrooms and 8 full baths), 22 in the carriage house (sharing 9 bedrooms and three baths), so 52 in all.
Dining: 40 in the large dining room, 25 in the breakfast room

LOCATION

Travel north on I-95 and take Exit 93 (Perryville-Port Deposit) immediately after paying the toll at the Susquehanna River Bridge. Turn left onto Route 222 and drive one-half mile to the flashing yellow light; turn left (this is still Route 222). Turn left again at the Mt. Ararat Farm DBC sign and follow the farm driveway to the Donaldson Brown Center.

FOOD/BEVERAGE

The staff here usually handles your food and beverage arrangements, and you should discuss your requirements with them. The cuisine focus is on "homemade regional dishes."

LIMITATIONS/RESTRICTIONS

The center is available all year at any time. The group who reserves the center has exclusive use of the site during its entire stay. The center's primary use is as a retreat site for groups pursuing educational or intellectual purposes. Children are not allowed. Food, beverages, and smoking are outlawed on the second floor of the mansion.

LEAD TIME FOR RESERVATIONS

Call for availability.

RATES

The center charges $99.50 per person per day, which covers costs for accommodations, three meals, and two breaks. You also may request cookouts and picnics; discuss rates for these with the center.

FACILITIES FOR THE PHYSICALLY HANDICAPPED?
YES NO SOME
X

A ramp and elevator allow access into and throughout the house. Bathrooms are large enough to accommodate wheelchairs but are not specially equipped.

HAMMOND-HARWOOD HOUSE

19 Maryland Avenue
Annapolis, Maryland 2140
410/269-1714

House from the "Golden Age of Annapolis"

If you'd been around Annapolis in the years 1760 to 1775, most likely you would have been caught up in the exciting swirl of cultural, social, and political activities that marked these years ever after as the "Golden Age of Annapolis." And if you had had money during this time, no doubt you would have commissioned a fine architect like William Buckland to build you an impressive house like the Hammond-Harwood.

Hammond-Harwood House is an elegant brick mansion of the late Georgian style, designed by Buckland (his last project before a tragic death) and built in 1774 for lawyer and planter Mathias Hammond, although he is thought never to have moved in. In addition to the superb architectural details, you'll marvel over the house's collection of late 18th- and early 19th-century decorative arts. You have the opportunity to do so—for a fee—when you hold an event here.

Functions take place in the museum kitchen and hyphen, the conference room, and the garden. The kitchen is on the first floor and overlooks Maryland Avenue through its semi-octagonal bay window. The original floor is brick, paved in an herringbone pattern. There's a large cooking fireplace and tons of brass, pewter, copper, wood, iron, and earthenware implements, all of the early 19th-century period. Across the granite-floored hyphen and down a set of steps is the conference room of stone and brick walls, and furnished with a heavy, long oak table. The garden features a large green lawn sloping back towards trees and shrubbery and boarded by boxwoods and an herb plot. Two brick

26

terraces extend off the hyphens on either side of the house, which projects between the two. The terraces may be tented.

CAPACITY

Reception: 50 in the conference room, 50 in the museum kitchen and hyphen, and 75 in the garden
Banquet: 24 in the kitchen, 30 in the conference room, and 24 outside on the terraces

LOCATION

From the Baltimore Beltway, (I-695), pick up I-97/Rt. 3 south and follow I-97 to Rt. 50, where you exit in the direction of Annapolis. Take Rt. 50 to the Rowe Boulevard (Rt. 70) exit and travel through three stop lights to the end; turn left onto College Avenue. Go to your first stop light and turn right onto King George Street, go one block and turn right onto Maryland Avenue. The Hammond-Harwood House is immediately on your left.

FOOD/BEVERAGE

The site has an approved caterers list; you may choose one not on the list subject to the site's approval. A limited kitchen is available off the museum kitchen.

LIMITATIONS/RESTRICTIONS

The house is available to members—you need only join for $25 (individuals) or $150 (businesses) to use it. You may rent the kitchen, hyphen, and garden Tuesday through Sunday from 4:30 P.M. to 9:30 P.M. during the months of November through March, from 5:30 P.M. to 9:30 P.M. during the months of April through October, and every Monday from 9:00 A.M. through 9:30 P.M. The conference room is generally available during the same times, but the museum's schedule takes precedence here. Smoking is allowed in the garden only. Amplified music is discouraged, and dancing is permitted on the terraces. Tenting on the lawn will be considered on a case-to-case basis.

LEAD TIME FOR RESERVATIONS
Call for availability.

RATES

Museum kitchen and hyphen: $125 for two hours, plus $30 for each additional hour.
Garden: $250 for two hours, plus $50 for each additional hour.
Museum kitchen, hyphen, and garden: $300 for two hours, plus $50 for each additional hour.
Conference Room: $200 for an all-day conference; if the conference takes place entirely within operating hours, the rate is $75 for two hours plus $25 for each additional hour; if the event takes place after regular hours, the fee is $100 for two hours and $30 for each additional hour. Individual membership fees run $25 per person, business memberships are $150 each, cleanup and security fees are $50, and group tour rates are $3.00 per adult, $1.50 per student.

FACILITIES FOR THE PHYSICALLY HANDICAPPED?
YES NO SOME
              X

The garden and terraces are accessible to wheelchairs, but not the restrooms.

MARYVALE CASTLE

Maryvale Preparatory School
11300 Falls Road
Brooklandville, Maryland 21022
410/252-3528

American manor house of Tudor style

It wasn't hyperbole that earned this grand stone manor house the title of "castle." The Wickes family, who built the place in 1917, modeled the building after Warwick Castle in England. Consequently, you'll see a porte-cochere at the entrance for carriages to pass under, sturdy, iron-studded doors, English Gothic arched windows, diamond-paned leaded-glass windows and doors, and all the authentic touches that truly turn a home into a castle.

In 1945, the Sisters of Notre Dame de Namur purchased the property, and the castle now serves as the central administration and classroom structure on the campus of Maryvale, an all-girls preparatory school. Happily, the sisters recognize the site's attributes as a compellingly dramatic event spot and let the public use certain first floor areas for functions.

Specifically, the Great Hall, library, solarium, chapel, terrace, and lawn are the special event spaces. The Great Hall is the most magnificent: molded plaster ceiling, European oak-paneled walls with Tudor-style carvings, baroque chairs, bay window, and diamond-paned leaded-glass doors opening to the terrace. The castle is situated on a hill so when you step out to the awning-covered flagstone terrace, you're looking down and out at the emerald green lawn and landscaped grounds heading back into the distance. The chapel is dark and paneled, the library has a Tudor-style ceiling and more paneling, and the solarium has a brick-tiled floor, stone walls, and an immense fireplace. For a few hours, for the right price, you and your merry band of revelers can be the keepers of this castle.

CAPACITY

Reception: 75 inside (November through April), 100 inside and on the terrace (May through October)
Banquet: 60 inside or out, no matter the time of year
Chapel service: 60, seated

LOCATION

From the Baltimore Beltway (I-695), take the Falls Road exit, headed north. Follow Falls Road until you come to Maryvale's entrance, on the left.

FOOD/BEVERAGE

You must choose your caterer from the school's approved list. There is a kitchen in the castle.

LIMITATIONS/RESTRICTIONS

The castle is available weekends and weekdays year-round, subject to the school's schedule. Events must end by 8:00 P.M. Smoking is permitted only on the terrace. There is limited space for dancing.

LEAD TIME FOR RESERVATIONS

Call at least a month in advance.

RATES

Wedding ceremony: $350.
Wedding ceremony and reception: $750 for a three-hour function, $775 for a three and one-half-hour function, and $800 for a four-hour function.
Reception only: $650 for a three-hour event, $675 for a three and one-half-hour event, and $700 for a four-hour event.
Call for rates for other functions.
You'll want to be sure when you book the castle for a function, since the site charges a hefty non-refundable deposit, about half the rental fee, to reserve your date.

FACILITIES FOR THE PHYSICALLY HANDICAPPED?
YES NO SOME
        X

The first floor is wheelchair-accessible; the restrooms are two steps up.

H.L. MENCKEN HOUSE

1524 Hollins Street
Baltimore, Maryland 21223
410/396-7997 or 396-8395

Henry's home for 68 years

An unassuming brick rowhouse facing Union Square pre-
serves the life and times of one of Baltimore's most noted
characters, the "Sage of Baltimore," Henry Louis Mencken.
Meet here and you'll see the man's treasured Tonk baby
grand piano, the sofa on which he and F. Scott Fitzgerald
(among others) sat imbibing Mencken's home-brewed beer
or stronger stuff, and the desk in the upstairs study where
Mencken composed many of his works.

You have the use of the garden and the entire downstairs—parlor, sitting room, and dining room—and viewing
privileges of the second floor study, when you stage a function here. Unlike most historic sites, the Mencken House
is user-friendly, that is, you may actually sit on the same
chairs and sofa where Mencken once sat, and dine at the
table where Mencken himself ate. Most of the furnishings
in these small rooms did belong to Mencken or to his family.

A brief filmstrip in the parlor fills you in little more on
the man. Still, if you're having a function here, it's worth
paying the $25 extra for a guide to tell you the best tidbits:
how Mencken came to amass a wonderful collection, for
example, or the significance of various objects in the garden.
The H.L. Mencken House is one of the six museums operated by the city's Baltimore City Life Museums (BCLM)
organization. (See the index to find the other properties:
the Peale Museum and Baltimore City Life Museums,
Museum Row Site...

CAPACITY
Reception
Banque

31

LOCATION

The house lies about two miles west of the Inner Harbor, off of Martin Luther King Jr. Boulevard.

FOOD/BEVERAGE

You may choose your own caterer and menu, subject to approval by the site manager. Caterers may use the small kitchen on the first floor. Heavy cooking in oils is prohibited.

LIMITATIONS/RESTRICTIONS

The museum is available for events after 4:00 P.M. in winter and after 5:00 P.M. in summer. BCLM corporate members receive preference on the use of the museum for special functions. Food and drink must be kept to the first floor of each site. Smoking is permitted outdoors only. Red wine is not allowed anywhere on the premises.

LEAD TIME FOR RESERVATIONS

At least a month in advance; reservations made more than six months ahead may be subject to change when BCLM programming takes precedence.

RATES

$100 an hour on weekdays or $150 an hour Friday through Sunday, plus expenses for security, guides, the house manager, and setup and breakdown. User fees for corporate members vary according to their level of membership.

FACILITIES FOR THE PHYSICALLY HANDICAPPED?
YES NO SOME
    X

WAYSIDE INN

4344 Columbia Road

Ellicott City, Maryland 21042

410/461-4636

Half way to Washington and right next to Columbia

Originally, this Federal-period stone house with its 18-inch-thick walls was a farmhouse. Built during the first half of the 19th century, the building presided over acres and acres of a plantation. You won't catch any chickens or cows wandering the grounds these days, though. The inn's property now covers all of two acres, just enough to lend the place a country feel, despite the fact that Rt. 29 is only a minute away.

The Wayside operates primarily as a bed-and-breakfast: its third floor holds two suites, each with its own sitting room, bedroom and private bath, while the two second floor guest rooms share a bath. The main rooms on the first floor are the cream and burgundy-colored parlor, the adjoining music room and across the front-to-back central hall, the dining room with its green-painted wainscoting and large bu.... Downstairs is the cozy tavern of exposed beams, stone w... and brick floor. Other attractions here include the work.. fireplaces (nine in all), the screened-in porch surveying... and other back lawn and pond, and the tasteful antiques which is a.shings all thr...gh the house. The Wayside, small-scale ditioned by th...ay, is a gracious spot for ...ining.

CAPACITY

Reception: 25

Meeting: 10 or fe...

Banquet (catered lu...

available when you'...r dinner): small &..

accommodations ... the entire inn, in...of 8 or so, ...overnight

Sites for
100 to 200 People

Debbie

BABE RUTH BIRTHPLACE AND BASEBALL CENTER

216 Emory Street
Baltimore, Maryland 21230
410/727-1539

Everything you ever wanted to know about baseball

If there's nothing that you want to know about baseball, better look elsewhere. But if the idea of hanging baseball jerseys, framed black-and-white photos of famous Orioles, and exhibits on such topics as "Famous Families of Baseball" excites you, 'dis is da place for youse. Technically, you don't have to be a baseball enthusiast to enjoy a party here—for example, you might want to choose Babe Ruth Birthplace for the sheer American feel of the place—but it does help.

In wall-to-wall carpeted rooms on both floors of this narrow brick townhouse, baseball memorabilia is crammed everywhere. There are pennants, there's an 1894 Hanlon Cup under glass, an exhibit on Maryland's Baseball Hall of Fame, 714 plaques on the wall commemorating each of Babe's career home runs, and a 25-minute documentary on George Herman ("Babe") Ruth himself.

At the back of the museum is a brick courtyard that can be tented. An unadorned basement room may be used for children's parties. By the All-Star game in 1993, the museum will have expanded to include a new and larger facility just down the street (and two blocks over from the Orioles' new stadium).

CAPACITY

Reception: 125
Banquet: 40
Children's party room: 20 kids

LOCATION

The house is located off of the 600 block of West Pratt Street and 1½ blocks from the new ball park.

FOOD/BEVERAGE

The site works exclusively with one caterer. There is a small kitchen on the premises.

LIMITATIONS/RESTRICTIONS

The house is available to adults after 4:00 P.M. November through March and after 5:00 P.M. April through October. The museum offers its basement room for children's parties during the day. Smoking is prohibited in the building. The site is really not large enough to accommodate either a band or dancing. Events end at midnight.

LEAD TIME FOR RESERVATIONS

Call six weeks in advance.

RATES

The museum charges a flat fee of $300 for pre-game parties and for events of up to 25 people, and $400 for all other functions. The kids' room goes for $35, plus $1 per child.

FACILITIES FOR THE PHYSICALLY HANDICAPPED?
YES NO SOME
    X

BALTIMORE PUBLIC WORKS MUSEUM

751 Eastern Avenue
Baltimore, Maryland 21202
410/396-1509

What goes on under your feet and above the street

In a magnificent, Edwardian, red brick building that houses the Eastern Avenue Pumping Station is this modest-sized museum that tells you the works about public works. Here you can learn how Baltimore has developed its municipal services that provide water, dispose of wastes, and build roads and bridges.

In a series of exhibits arranged circularly on the first level of this open, multi-story-high boiler room, you discover where Baltimore gets its water (from three rivers), the dangers and development of tunneling, the women who have played a significant role in public works, and interesting info about what's going on beneath our streets: the non-stop actions of gas, electric, freshwater supply, waste-water disposal, steam, and storm-water systems.

This is a non-glamorous spot, where decoration includes exposed pipes and coal bins, painted concrete blocks, and brown carpeting. But the subject is fascinating and bound to stimulate conversation among the shyest of your gathering. In good weather, you can use the museum's "Streetscape," a fenced-in outside area that features a larger-than-life size model of public works pipes.

CAPACITY

Reception: 200
Banquet: 100
Meeting: up to 50
Streetscape: up to 200

LOCATION

The museum is located between President Street and East Falls Avenue, right on the Jones Falls Canal, on the Little Italy side of the Inner Harbor.

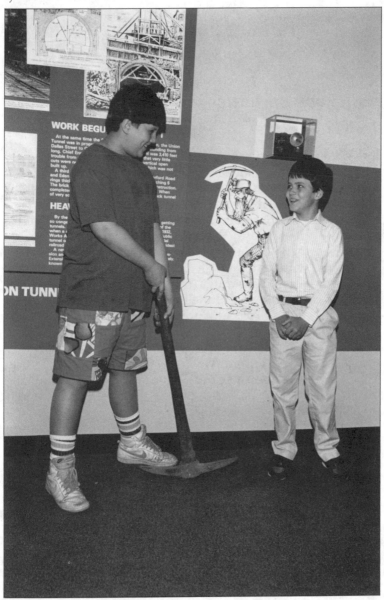

Photo: Ralph Kueppers

FOOD/BEVERAGE

You may choose your own caterer, subject to approval by the museum. A small kitchen on site offers a microwave, a stove, an oven, a refrigerator, and a sink.

LIMITATIONS/RESTRICTIONS

Smoking is not permitted in the building. The museum is available for events at any time.

LEAD TIME FOR RESERVATIONS

Call at least 30 days ahead.

RATES

$500 for nonmembers, $250 for members.

FACILITIES FOR THE PHYSICALLY HANDICAPPED?
YES NO SOME
                X

A handicapped entrance at the back of the museum allows guests in wheelchairs access to the museum. The restrooms can accommodate wheelchairs but aren't specially equipped.

BROOM HALL

2425 Pocock Road

Fallston, Maryland 21047

410/557-7321 or 1/800/552-3965

Modern bed-and-breakfast modeled after old English manor house

Although just 20 years old, Broom Hall captures some of the spirit of a centuries-old English manor. Twelve-foot-high ceilings, hardwood floors, English antique furniture, and paintings and photographs of proper British gentlemen and movie-star gorgeous women catch the eye inside; an English garden allee, a pond, and rolling hills dotted with trees enchant the viewer outdoors.

Broom Hall was built by the current owner's grandparents, a British general and his beautiful American wife, to replicate on a small scale the family's original Broom Hall estate in England.

First floor rooms (drawing and dining rooms, library, and foyer) and the back lawn are available for private functions, or you can take over the whole house, including the five private bedrooms, for overnight business retreats or to house wedding guests. All rooms are tastefully furnished, while conveying a pleasant hominess.

CAPACITY

Reception: 75 inside
Banquet: 25 inside
Picnic/lawn party: 150, with the use of a tent
Overnight accommodations: 5 bedrooms with private baths

LOCATION

From the Baltimore Beltway (I-695), exit north on Dulaney Valley Road (Rt. 146) and travel 15 miles to Pocock Road. Take a right on Pocock Road; Broom Hall is the last driveway on the

*right. From I-95, exit north on Rt. 152 and travel
approximately 12 miles to Pocock Road. Turn left onto Pocock
Road and left again into the first driveway.*

FOOD/BEVERAGE

*You may choose your own caterer, although the site can
recommend area caterers, if you wish. The caterer has access to
the bed-and-breakfast's fully equipped kitchen and butler's
pantry.*

LIMITATIONS/RESTRICTIONS

*Smoking is permitted outside only. The inn is available any
time for private functions.*

LEAD TIME FOR RESERVATIONS

*Book your event a year in advance for weekends in September
and October and April through June; otherwise call as soon as
you have a date in mind.*

RATES

*Rates range from $350 to $650 for four-hour functions. Guest
rooms run $80 to $125 a night. Honeymoon/anniversary
packages are available for $25 extra per night.*

FACILITIES FOR THE PHYSICALLY HANDICAPPED?
YES NO SOME
           X

*A ramp at the front door allows access to the first floor's foyer
and two bedrooms with private baths; however, three steps lead
down from the foyer to the other main floor rooms.*

CARROLL COUNTY FARM MUSEUM

500 South Center Street
Westminster, Maryland 21157
410/876-2667 or 1/800/654-4645

Two pavilions and a glimpse of life down on the farm

For an old-fashioned good time hold your event at this farm, which re-creates life as it was lived in the late 19th century.

A tour of the Carroll County Farm Museum will take you through six rooms of the 1853 brick mansion (operated as an almshouse until 1965), outbuildings (including a smoke house, spring house, and blacksmith shop), an herb and flower garden, exhibit barns housing old farm memorabilia such as threshing and harvesting equipment, and past the sheds for a lively bunch of farm animals.

Your party takes place in one of the farm's two modern-day structures: covered pavilions, both of which have concrete floors, arched wood ceilings, and scores of picnic tables with attached benches. The "inner" pavilion, which stands off to the side of the mansion, offers a partly sheltered stage area. The "outer" pavilion lies closer to the road, at a little distance from the house and outbuildings. The open-sided pavilions let you take in bucolic views of open pastures, barns, and woodlands as your own event unfolds.

CAPACITY

Reception or banquet: 100 to 150 in either pavilion

LOCATION

From the Baltimore Beltway (I-695), take Exit 19 to I-795. Follow I-795 to Rt. 140 west to Westminster. When you reach Westminster, turn left onto Center Street from Rt. 140, and follow Center Street around to the farm.

FOOD/BEVERAGE

You handle your own catering arrangements. Neither of the pavilions has a kitchen, but both are equipped with water and electricity hookups. Grills are permitted; alcohol is not.

LIMITATIONS/RESTRICTIONS

Pets are not allowed. Live bands and tents must be approved of in advance. The music must be in keeping with the atmosphere of the farm (i.e. no rock music allowed). The pavilions are available in April, Tuesday through Friday, from 10:00 A.M. to 4:00 P.M.; and May through October, Tuesday through Friday, from 10:00 A.M. to 4:00 P.M., Saturday and Sunday, from 12:00 NOON to 5:00 P.M.

LEAD TIME FOR RESERVATIONS

Call six weeks in advance.

RATES

$25 for the use of either pavilion. To tour the mansion and exhibit buildings you pay these admission prices: group rate—$2 per person when your group numbers 20 or more; for groups of fewer than 20 people—$3 per adult, $2 per child (ages 6-18) and adults over 60, and under six, free.

FACILITIES FOR THE PHYSICALLY HANDICAPPED?
YES NO SOME
X

CLOISTERS CHILDREN'S MUSEUM

10440 Falls Road
Brooklandville, Maryland 21022
410/823-2551

A stone castle in a fairy tale setting

The densely wooded acres surrounding the Cloisters Children's Museum could be where Robin Hood and his gang hung out, or where Sleeping Beauty lived with the three fairies until her 16th birthday. The museum, itself, could be the castle where Cinderella met her prince. Talk to anyone in Baltimore about unusual and magical places to have parties, and the first site that's mentioned is most often the Cloisters.

Despite its appearance of medieval glory, the massive stone building was completed in the early 1930s. Owners Sumner and Dudrea Parker designed the home to reflect the centuries-old French and English architecture they had seen in their European travels. The castle's interior continues the Middle Ages theme in its use of stone supports, walls, and doorways and in its preponderance of dark and decorative woodwork.

Your event takes place on the first floor of the castle. Throughout the gallery, living room, library, and buffet area are mullioned windows, huge hearths, oak, walnut and chestnut wall and ceiling beams, and large, ornately carved antiques. Furniture stands along the walls or in corners, leaving each room plenty of party space. You'll notice the abundance of European and American paintings, dating from the 17th through the 19th centuries. If you're planning a late fall or winter function, you'll be happy to know that the museum allows you to get a roaring fire going in that mammoth living room fireplace. Those scheduling a spring fling are welcome to use the patio and front lawn.

CAPACITY

Reception: 175
Banquet: 80
Meeting: 80 to 100

LOCATION

From the Baltimore Beltway (I-695) headed north, take Exit 23B (Falls Road), and travel to the first traffic light, where you turn

left onto Falls Road. Proceed a half-mile to the museum driveway.

FOOD/BEVERAGE

You may choose any licensed caterer, and the site has a list of recommended caterers, if that will help. There is a non-commercial kitchen on the premises, which may be used for warming and preparation work, but not for cooking.

LIMITATIONS/RESTRICTIONS

The museum is available for special events from 6:00 P.M. to midnight seven days a week, all year except for the summer months (mid-June through the beginning of September). Smoking, music and dancing are allowed. Candles are permitted when they are placed on dinner tables or used as part of a wedding ceremony. Throwing of rice is not allowed.

LEAD TIME FOR RESERVATIONS

The museum books events up to a year in advance.

RATES

Weekend events: $700; Monday through Thursday functions: $500; December events, regardless of the day of the week: $700. In addition, the museum requires that you hire at least two of their security guards to supervise your event, at $85 for each guard.

FACILITIES FOR THE PHYSICALLY HANDICAPPED?
YES NO SOME
X

DAVIDGE HALL

522 West Lombard Street
Baltimore, Maryland 21201
410/328-7454

A *haunting monument to medical history*

Ooh-h-h. People say ghosts roam the passages and chambers of Davidge Hall, and you can believe them. The brick building was erected by the University of Maryland Medical School as a teaching facility in 1812, and the place fairly resonates with the spirit and experiences of the many students who listened to lectures, dissected cadavers (an innovative albeit illegal practice until 1880), and performed chemical experiments here.

Having said all that, let me add a caveat: Davidge Hall is fascinating, not scary. Eight thick, white doric columns and a portico give its facade a Parthenon-like appearance, while the turreted main body of the structure resembles the Pantheon in Rome. Two large amphitheaters reside, one above the other, inside the dome. Chemical Hall is on the first level, a two-story-high, semi-circular room with tiers of built-in wooden seats rising above the central lecturing space. Students performed their chemical experiments using the series of furnaces you see set in the wall at the front of the hall. Directly above lies Anatomical Hall, a smaller amphitheater and brighter, thanks to the skylight dome. These two rooms, the foyer and a side rose garden are the rental areas.

CAPACITY

Reception: 150 in Chemical Hall and the adjoining foyer, 50 in Anatomical Hall, 100 in the rose garden
Banquet: 70 in Chemical Hall and adjoining foyer, 40 in the rose garden. Note: remember the layout of Chemical Hall—its

tiers of seats—and forget ideas about rows of banquet tables and traditional setups.

Lecture: 208 in Chemical Hall, 100 in Anatomical Hall

LOCATION

Across from University Hospital in downtown Baltimore, between Greene and Paca streets, on West Lombard Street.

FOOD/BEVERAGE

You must choose your caterer from the site's approved list. The site also reserves the right to approve your menu. (Certain smells, like crab, tend to linger for days here, much to the distress of employees of the University of Maryland Medical Alumni Association, who have offices in the building.) There is a small kitchen equipped with a sink, stove, ice-maker, dishwasher, and refrigerator.

LIMITATIONS/RESTRICTIONS

Smoking is prohibited. Food and drinks are not permitted in Anatomical Hall. Also, you should know that Anatomical Hall's acoustics are rather, um, interesting, its heating system rather, um, weak, and its electrical hookups actually nonexistent.

LEAD TIME FOR RESERVATIONS

Call for availability.

RATES

Students and faculty of the University of Maryland at Baltimore may use Davidge Hall for free. Outside groups pay $350 for a weekday event, $400 for a Saturday or Sunday function. These rates cover a four-hour period; you pay $50 for each additional hour.

FACILITIES FOR THE PHYSICALLY HANDICAPPED?
YES NO SOME
X

JOHN H. DOWNS MEMORIAL PARK

8311 John Downs Loop
Pasadena, Maryland 21122
410/222-6230

A county park on the Chesapeake Bay

Parks are for picnics, sure enough, but here's a park that also offers sites for weddings and other un-picnic-like events. Downs Park's 231 acres include three pavilions and a "Mother's Garden."

The Mother's Garden, situated near the park's information center, was originally part of a summer estate belonging to the Thom family. Thom's wife is said to have planted the plot in the early 1900s. The garden is separated into small flower beds connected by a brick walkway. Down the center of the garden, a trellis overgrown with greenery provides a shaded path to the back. There's a sweep of green lawn to one side, where you may set up chairs for your guests. Wedding ceremonies frequently take place between the two large trees at the front of this lawn or in the small gazebo beyond this area.

The three pavilions scattered elsewhere on the campus serve as locations for wedding receptions, outdoorsy business meetings, and sundry other occasions. Each of the pavilions has a concrete floor, wood coved roof, and 17 picnic tables with benches attached. One of the pavilions has a big stone fireplace at one end. Volleyball nets and grills lie near the pavilions.

In addition, the park offers 7½ miles of hiking and biking trails, tennis, handball, and basketball courts, softball diamonds, a playground, and bay overlooks of the park's 2,000 feet of Chesapeake frontage.

CAPACITY

Reception: up to 125 in each of the pavilions
Banquet: up to 100 in each of the pavilions

Wedding ceremony: up to 100, seated, on the lawn of the Mother's Garden

LOCATION

From Baltmore, take the Baltimore Beltway (I-695) south to Rt. 3 south to Rt. 100 east, to Rt. 177 east (Mountain Road), to the park.

FOOD/BEVERAGE

You choose your own caterer. Only keg beer is allowed—no wine or hard liquor. To serve beer, you must obtain a permit from the Anne Arundel County Department of Recreation and Parks, who runs the park. There is no kitchen.

LIMITATIONS/RESTRICTIONS

The pavilions and Mother's Garden are rentable from 9:00 A.M. to dusk, year-round, Wednesday through Monday. The Mother's Garden is available only as a wedding site. The park provides no electricity or running water for the pavilions but will provide electricity for wedding ceremonies in the Mother's Garden. Amplified sound is not allowed in the park.

LEAD TIME FOR RESERVATIONS

The park starts accepting reservations on January 1 for the year's calendar. Call in January to reserve one of the pavilions. Call in January or February to reserve the Mother's Garden for a May or June wedding; otherwise the timing is not so crucial.

RATES

Pavilion: $100 (Anne Arundel County residents), $200 (outside groups). Additional fees: $50 for keg beer permit, per car parking costs ($4 for county residents, $6 for others). Mother's Garden: $100 (no additional fees required).

FACILITIES FOR THE PHYSICALLY HANDICAPPED?
YES NO SOME
        X

The pavilions are at ground level, but access to them is grass, not paved. The Mother's Garden is flat grass but not paved. The restrooms are handicapped accessible.

GOVERNMENT HOUSE

1129 North Calvert Street
Baltimore, Maryland 21202
410/396-3755

Where the city entertains distinguished visitors, and so can you

Government House is a gorgeous city-owned Victorian property that the mayor uses to entertain visiting dignitaries, but the building serves other functions, too. The upper floors operate as a bed-and-breakfast—Baltimoreans planning to pursue careers in the hospitality business can train here. And Government House is open to the public as an impressive site for small meetings and social gatherings.

Constructed in 1889 by Baltimore businessman John Gilman, the house has also been the home of other renowned Baltimoreans. The city first acquired the building in 1939, and then its two adjoining row houses, and performed a major re-haul in 1983 that produced the exquisite, 19th-century, Victorian-style interior you see today.

Throughout the first floor rental space are polished parquet floors partly overthrown with colorful flowered rugs; Victorian, etched globe chandeliers; high ceilings; a preponderance of maroon and gold in the William Morris wallpaper and in the heavy drapes; and lots of finely crafted woodwork. Rooms off the central, mahogany-paneled hall are the reception room, a favorite spot for wedding ceremonies; a parlor, with a Japanese fan represented in the ceiling's wallpaper and a bay window overlooking Calvert Street; the long dining room with its long table, and an 1841 chandelier whose base is actually knights-in-armor figures curving upward; and a small butler's pantry with an elaborate sideboard that serves as an excellent place to display a wedding cake.

At the rear of the central hall is the library, most handsomely appointed in English oak paneling, leaded-glass

54

windows with stained-glass filaments, and a large bay window and built-in, cushioned seat below it.

CAPACITY

Reception: 100
Banquet: 50
Meeting: 30

LOCATION

Government House lies at the corner of Biddle and Calvert streets in downtown Baltimore, about a mile up from the Inner Harbor. A maroon awning over its entrance displays in bold letters the words "Government House."

FOOD/BEVERAGE

You choose your own licensed and insured caterer. The first floor holds a large, fully equipped kitchen.

LIMITATIONS/RESTRICTIONS

Smoking and dancing are not permitted, and loud music is not encouraged, since bed-and-breakfast guests are just upstairs. The site is available every day, all day.

LEAD TIME FOR RESERVATIONS

The site prefers that you call at least a month in advance.

RATES

Rates vary, depending upon the intended length of your party, how many people are coming, whether you serve food, and whether it's a seated event. At the low end of the range, nonprofit organizations pay $50 for a four-hour event for up to 12 guests where no food is served. At the high end, an individual or corporate visitor pays $600 for a three-hour cocktail reception for 76 to 100 guests.

FACILITIES FOR THE PHYSICALLY HANDICAPPED?
YES NO SOME
X

HAMPTON MANSION TEAROOM AND TERRACE

535 Hampton Lane
Towson, Maryland 21204
410/583-7401

Where history and beauty abound

Poor Captain Ridgely. No sooner had the man completed his Georgian jewel of a mansion in 1790 than he died. The man who had made his fortune from a number of enterprises, farming, ironworks, and merchandising among them, left behind a 2,000-acre estate that included not only the 33-room dwelling but stables, an overseer's house, slave quarters, a dairy, barns, many exotic trees, and beautiful landscaped grounds. Fortunately, Ridgely also left behind some family. Ridgelys occupied Hampton Mansion, tended the property, and added their own touches—an orangerie, formal gardens, greenhouses—until the 1940s.

Now a historic site administered by the National Park Service, Hampton Mansion is available as a party spot, too. To be exact, the mansion's tearoom and adjoining terrace may be used for functions. You may tour the manor and wander all over the estate, but you must confine your food and drink setups, tables and chairs, tent, music, and decorations to the tearoom/terrace area.

The tearoom, located at the end of the house's left wing, is snug, painted in shades of Williamsburg blue and white, and features a huge hearth, a combination brick and broad-beamed wood floor, and expansive windows. A door leads directly outside to the terrace, where hedges, trees, and a little garden border the brick courtyard and its neighboring grass plot. This area is private and allows a view of the back lawn.

By all means, take a look around while you're here. Inside the mansion you'll find furnishings that reflect the entire Ridgely residency; outside are immense cedar of Lebanon trees, catalpas and magnolias, and tiered parterres sloping back towards a woods.

CAPACITY

Reception: 200
Banquet: 150

LOCATION

From the Baltimore Beltway (I-695), take Exit 27 and go north on Dulaney Valley Road to Hampton Lane. Take a right onto Hampton Lane, which leads to the park. (Be careful not to enter the Beltway ramps located just before the turnoff for Hampton Lane.)

FOOD/BEVERAGE

You handle the liquor arrangements and, for wedding receptions, the wedding cake. The mansion takes care of the catering, which is standard American fare. Hampton provides ice, glasses, cocktail napkins, bartenders, waiters, linens, tables, and chairs.

LIMITATIONS/RESTRICTIONS

The tearoom/terrace is available for four-hour periods, from April through October, 9:00 A.M. to 9:00 P.M., Tuesdays through Sundays. Amplified music is prohibited. You must have a minimum of 50 guests to reserve the site.

LEAD TIME FOR RESERVATIONS

Call six to seven months in advance.

RATES

There is no rental charge for the site. Catering costs range from $10 to $25 per person, plus 5 percent tax and 15 percent gratuity, depending upon your menu choices. You are not required to rent a tent, but they are available, at $300 for a 20-by-20-foot size, $450 for a 20-by-40-foot size, and $775 for a 30-by-50-foot tent.

FACILITIES FOR THE PHYSICALLY HANDICAPPED?
YES NO SOME
X

KENT MANOR INN

500 Kent Manor Drive
Stevensville, Kent Island, Maryland 21666
410/643-5757

A comfortable refuge overlooking a creek

Two hundred-odd acres of farmland and a swath of creek can add up to a mighty picturesque location, as various astute individuals have noted since this property was first charted in 1651. One such person built the original, three-story farmhouse in 1820, happy to keep the place his own private domain. Other owners have thought to share their enjoyment of the plantation by offering it as a summer hotel. The property's current owner goes that much further by presenting to the public an elegant inn and restaurant, meeting rooms, and separate garden house for special functions.

A Victorian decor prevails throughout the inn, from the elaborate window treatments in the dining rooms to the reproduction furniture in each of the 24 guest rooms. Some of the house's 1865 features remain, such as the fireplaces, each with Italian marble mantels, and the windowseats. The two meeting rooms are actually private dining rooms and so are absent of the "conference room" feel. Business execs can unwind from their off-site sessions by hiking, swimming, playing golf or horseshoes, or antiquing in area shops.

Across the lawn from the inn is the garden house. This octagonal building is a one-room, one-level pavilion with floor-to-ceiling windows on five sides. The room has a dance floor, bar, gray wall-to-wall carpeting, a center skylight, and ceiling fans. A cupola atop the skylight matches the eight-windowed cupola on the roof of the inn.

CAPACITY

Reception: 25 in the parlor (preceding a sit-down banquet), 175 in the garden house, 175 using the grounds (tent highly advised)
Banquet: up to 30 inside, 150 in the garden house
Meeting: up to 22 in one meeting room, 12 in the other; 150 in the garden house
Overnight accommodations: 24 guest rooms that can sleep a total of 60 people

LOCATION

From I-95, pick up Rt. 50 east towards the Bay Bridge. Just over the bridge, take your first exit labeled "Romancoke/ Stevensville," and turn right onto Rt. 8 South. Travel Rt. 8 for 200 yards and turn left onto Kent Manor Drive. Follow the one-mile drive all the way to the inn. Note: The Bay Bridge Airport is just across Rt. 8 from the inn.

FOOD/BEVERAGE

The inn handles all your food and beverage arrangements, including alcohol. (The inn is required by law to provide the alcohol for events, rather than allow guests to provide it.) The cuisine emphasis is on seafood, with special attention paid as well to beef and veal dishes.

LIMITATIONS/RESTRICTIONS

The inn is available for special events every day but Christmas, year-round. Smoking, music, and dancing are permitted. Children under eight are not allowed in the inn unless you've booked the whole inn.

LEAD TIME FOR RESERVATIONS

Call for availability.

RATES

Call for rates, which vary based on a number of factors, including type of event and when the event is scheduled.

FACILITIES FOR THE PHYSICALLY HANDICAPPED?
YES NO SOME
X

LIRIODENDRON

502 West Gordon Street
Bel Air, Maryland 21014
Baltimore: 410/879-4424
Harford County: 410/838-3942

Summer retreat for renowned Hopkins doctor

In the 1890s, Dr. Howard Kelly had a thriving medical career (he helped found the Johns Hopkins Medical College), a burgeoning family (in all, Kelly had nine children), and a German-born wife who missed her summers spent in Palladian-style Prussian villas.

What the good doctor needed was a summer home, a place that would not just offer the Kelly clan a respite from city heat, but also soothe his wife's homesick soul. He built Liriodendron.

The word liriodendron is the botanical name for the tulip poplar tree, of which there are many scattered about this nearly 100-acre property. The grounds, themselves, are fetching: wide lawns shaded by tall trees shielded by woodlands that thoroughly cut off the estate from the outside world.

In the middle of all this sits the mansion, a white, Palladian-style (naturally), 16-room dwelling with columns and covered porches of dramatic proportions. The main-event spaces downstairs are a 26-foot-wide center hall, the drawing room, and the dining room. The large chambers give on to each other through arched entryways and have soft wood floors and fireplaces. French doors in both the drawing and dining rooms take you out to the porticos. This floor also holds memorabilia libraries where you can learn more about Kelly. Up the grand staircase in the center hall is the skylight-lit second floor, including a small, pale-yellow meeting room furnished with Kelly's original dining room suite, a bridal room, and gallery spaces. (The Liriod-endron Foundation uses these rooms, which are closed during your event, to exhibit works of area artists.)

CAPACITY

Reception: 150 inside, up to 200 using the covered porches
Banquet: 100 inside, up to 200 using the outside porches

LOCATION

From the city, take I-95 north to Exit 77B, which leads you to Rt. 24. Follow Rt. 24 five miles to Rt. 1 and turn right. At the third traffic light, turn left onto Atwood Road; follow Atwood to Gordon Street and turn left. Gordon Street takes you to Liriodendron.

FOOD/BEVERAGE

You choose your own licensed caterer. A spacious, three-room kitchen holds a commercial stove, a refrigerator, and counter space.

LIMITATIONS/RESTRICTIONS

The site is available year-round at any time except Sundays, from 1:00 P.M. to 4:00 P.M., when it is open to the public for

tours. Tents are not allowed. Smoking is prohibited inside, amplified music is prohibited outside, and food and drink are not allowed upstairs.

LEAD TIME FOR RESERVATIONS

Call as soon as you have a date in mind.

RATES

The site charges $100 per hour for social events, $75 to $100 per hour for other types of functions. A corporate membership (costing $250 annually) allows members to rent the estate for less, about $50 an hour.

FACILITIES FOR THE PHYSICALLY HANDICAPPED?
YES NO SOME
X

LONDON TOWN PUBLIK HOUSE AND GARDENS

839 Londontown Road
Edgewater, Maryland 21037
410/222-1919

Flora and woodlands along the South River

Hard to imagine, but back in the mid-18th century this bluff on the South River was a bustling seaport for the townsite of London. The statuesque brick house that looks down on the river is all that lives on from those earlier days. Built in the 1760s as a lodge for ferry passengers, the old inn in recent years has been restored to give you a glimpse of the furnishings and activities typical of colonial times.

The Publick House, itself, is not the party site, although you may wander around the outside of the mansion while you're here. The real action takes place in the gardens adjacent to the pub: 10 acres of trails and open areas, and native and exotic plant species including 20,000 narcissus, primroses, peonies, and other early flowering perennials in spring, ornamental bark and colorful foliage in winter, and American wildflowers.

You can use one of four locations in the garden for small wedding ceremonies: the holly bay, gazebo, winter garden, or visitors center overlook. The visitors center building/pavilion/lawn is the only spot where you may have food and drink. Inside the center are a meeting room, restrooms, and kitchen. Extending off the back of the center is a large covered wooden deck—the pavilion. Beyond the deck is a healthy slice of green lawn hedged by the encroaching woodlands and, on one side, an open wooden platform permitting a view of the water. Guests are free to amble throughout the woodlands as they please.

CAPACITY

Wedding ceremonies: 15 in the holly bay garden, 30 in the gazebo environs, 50 in the winter garden, and 50 to 200 on the visitors center lawn
Reception: 200, using the tented lawn, the pavilion and the small meeting room in the visitors center
Banquet: 75 to 80 on the tented lawn outside the visitors center
Meeting: 65 to 70 in the meeting room

LOCATION

From the Baltimore Beltway (I-695) headed east towards Glen Burnie, take the exit for I-97/Rt. 3 going south. Stay on I-97 and exit onto Patuxent Boulevard (Rt. 665). Follow Rt. 665 to Rt. 2 south (Solomons Island Road), and turn right. Go across the South River Bridge, proceed to the second traffic light, and turn left onto Mayo Road. Go to the next traffic light and turn left onto Londontown Road; follow the road to the end and into the parking lot of the gardens.

FOOD/BEVERAGE

You must choose a caterer from the site's preferred list. There is a kitchen in the visitors center.

LIMITATIONS/RESTRICTIONS

The garden is available from mid-April to mid-October, Saturday from 10:00 A.M. to 8:00 P.M., and on Sunday, from NOON to 8:00 P.M., except for the months of April, October and November, when you must be out by 7:00 P.M. The garden is also available weekdays for small luncheons and tours. Food and drink and smoking are not permitted in the gardens. The site recommends that you rent their 20-by-40-foot tent when you have a group of 75 or more in your party.

LEAD TIME FOR RESERVATIONS

Call for availability. The site can't book dates further than a year in advance.

RATES

Call for rates.

FACILITIES FOR THE PHYSICALLY HANDICAPPED?
YES NO SOME
X

MARYLAND INN

16 Church Circle

Annapolis, Maryland 21401

Annapolis: 410/263-2641, Baltimore: 410/269-0990

Maryland: 800/847-8882, FAX: 301/268-3813

A "house of entertainment" from the get-go

The Maryland Inn has never made any bones about what it sees as its primary purpose: a "house of entertainment" is how its owner described the place in 1782 and, by golly, that's how the inn sees itself today.

The building's age, 215 years, and history—it has long been a popular meeting spot for eminent national, state, and military leaders—provide an intriguing flavor to functions held here.

In appearance, the inn pays main tribute to its 18th-century origins, although certain features, for instance, the mansard roof, the porches and lobby, recall the Victorian era. On the first floor, two rooms are available for events. The Anne Arundel Room is small, wallpapered in pale gold, carpeted in gray, and furnished with a chandelier, fireplace, and burgundy and gold drapes. Through the door lies the Duke of Gloucester Room, a long chamber of dusty rose-colored walls, Williamsburg-blue wainscoting, and large mirrors. Functions in these two rooms may overflow to the rounded entry hall.

Below stairs is the Crown and Crab Room, with blue-paneled and burgundy-striped wallpapered walls, track lights, and a hunt theme. The King of France Tavern, where soldiers hid during the American Revolution, is dark and comfortable, enclosed by the original stone and brick walls, and paved with painted brick.

The inn is also known for its fine restaurant and accommodations. There are 43 guest rooms.

65

CAPACITY

Reception: 155 using both main floor rooms, 120 using the downstairs rooms
Banquet: 90 using both main floor rooms, 80 using the downstairs rooms
Overnight accommodations: 43 guest rooms

LOCATION

From the Baltimore Beltway (I-695), take I-97 south to Rt. 50 south headed towards Annapolis. Exit at Rowe Boulevard/ Rt. 70, and follow the boulevard to College Avenue, where you turn right. This will take you directly in to Church Circle and the Maryland Inn.

FOOD/BEVERAGE

The inn handles all of your catering arrangements.

LIMITATIONS/RESTRICTIONS

The Anne Arundel and Duke of Gloucester rooms are available at any time. The Crown and Crab is available anytime Monday through Thursday, during the day on Friday and Saturday, and after 3:00 P.M. on Sundays. The King of France Tavern may be used on Tuesday and Wednesday evenings and weekdays at lunchtime. Smoking is permitted at the inn. The inn can arrange for valet parking, or you can park at the public parking garage on Main Street.

LEAD TIME FOR RESERVATIONS

Call a few months in advance.

RATES

The inn charges no rental fees for the rooms. Catering costs start at $13 per person for lunch and $20 per person for dinner.

FACILITIES FOR THE PHYSICALLY HANDICAPPED?
YES NO SOME
   X

MOUNT WASHINGTON CONFERENCE CENTER

5801 Smith Avenue

Baltimore, Maryland 21209

410/578-7694

FAX: 410/578-4213

Winning combination of old and new, work and play, city and country

The Mount Washington Conference Center is a complex of three interconnecting buildings, the oldest of which was built in 1855, the most recent in 1984. Located on 68 gorgeous acres whose green hills and woods include a gazebo, reflecting pond, and jogging and exercise path, the center is only a 15-minute drive from the Inner Harbor. Mount Washington offers all the makings for a successful meeting—conference and lecture rooms of varying sizes, equipment of every description—and sweetens the deal with plenty of post-meeting diversions: indoor basketball/volleyball court, heated indoor swimming pool, health center, and game room.

Once the site of an institute for girls, a hospital during the Civil War, and a grade school/high school/college campus, Mt. Washington became a training center for employees of the United States Fidelity and Guaranty (USF&G) insurance corporation in the 1980s, when USF&G bought and restored the buildings. Mt. Washington opened its doors to outside groups in February of 1985.

The conference center prides itself on providing a high quality retreat. Each guest room is furnished with a color TV and VCR, alarm clock/radio, private balcony looking over the grounds, and desks that extend the entire length of one wall. You gather for meals in one of two attractive dining rooms, one of which offers a sweeping view of the campus. Each conference room has comfortable chairs and extra-wide tables, along with the latest in audiovisual and other equipment. The center even employs a full-time recreation director to help you decide how to spend your leisure time!

CAPACITY

Conferences: from 5 to 130
Overnight accommodations: 48 bedrooms that can accommodate up to 92 people
Dining: up to 300

LOCATION

The conference center is situated on the outskirts of Baltimore City. From the Baltimore Beltway, take Exit 23 to the Jones Falls Expressway (I-83), headed south. Take Exit 10 on I-83 and get on Northern Parkway going east. Immediately after exiting, get into your far left lane. Turn left on Falls Road and travel four-tenths of a mile to Kelly Avenue. Turn left. Travel a

short distance and bear to the right at Greely Avenue, then cross Smith Avenue and enter the gates of the conference center.

FOOD/BEVERAGE

The conference center contracts with its own food service company to provide all your meals. There are two dining rooms, one formal and one rather less formal. You may also arrange for catered working lunches.

LIMITATIONS/RESTRICTIONS

The center is available year-round to corporate, medical, educational, and other groups. At the time this book was researched, the facility was not rentable for social events unconnected to a scheduled conference. Smoking is permitted only in designated hotel rooms and in the outdoor courtyard.

LEAD TIME FOR RESERVATIONS

Call for availability.

RATES

Weekday rates are $155 for a single room, $185 for a double room. Weekend rates are $110 for a single room, $160 for a double room. These rates cover meals and coffee breaks and complete conference center services. When you reserve fewer than 10 guest rooms, or when you schedule a non-residential day meeting, you pay for use of the conference rooms, which run from $125 to $300 per room per day. The meal package rate for day meetings is about $20.95 per person, which includes breakfast, lunch, and two coffee breaks.

FACILITIES FOR THE PHYSICALLY HANDICAPPED?
YES NO SOME
X

NATIONAL MUSEUM OF CERAMIC ART

250 West Pratt Street
Baltimore, Maryland 21201
410/837-2529

Ceramic art in a contemporary setting

Baltimore's newest art museum, the only one of its kind in the country, showcases ceramic works created by local, national, and international artists, past and contemporary masters alike. The museum is a bright, single room gallery located on the lobby level of an office building. Gray wall-to-wall carpeting engulfs the floor and white paint covers the walls. Floor-to-ceiling glass walls on three sides of the tall chamber let in natural filtered light and capture background shots of Pratt and South Howard streets. Track lights pinpoint the works, which are exhibited throughout the room in glass cases, on pedestals, and on the walls. At any given time, you might find vases, pots, plates, whimsical pieces, and assorted other objects made from a variety of mediums: clay, stoneware, earthenware, slate, porcelain, glass, terra cotta, or a composite of these elements. One exhibit might feature "Pueblo Pottery of the Southwest," while another highlights the designs of regional artists. The combination of the intriguing art and the airy chamber make the museum a pleasant place to entertain.

CAPACITY

Reception: 35 to 135
These numbers are approximate since the amount of space available for a party really depends upon how much space is taken up by a particular exhibit.

LOCATION

The museum is two blocks west of the Inner Harbor, across from the Baltimore Convention Center and the new Oriole Stadium.

71

FOOD/BEVERAGE

You may choose your own caterer, subject to the approval of the museum. There is no kitchen on-site.

LIMITATIONS/RESTRICTIONS

The museum is available anytime on Monday and after 4:00 P.M. Tuesday through Sunday, year-round. Smoking is prohibited. The museum allows you to hold events here with the understanding that your group must not touch or endanger the art in any way.

LEAD TIME FOR RESERVATIONS

Call at least a month or two in advance.

RATES

The museum charges a non-refundable $200 fee to reserve the space, plus an agreed-upon per-person fee.

FACILITIES FOR THE PHYSICALLY HANDICAPPED?
YES NO SOME
X

OVERHILLS MANSION

916 South Rolling Road
Catonsville, Maryland 21228
410/744-0040

First owner's wedding gift makes an admirable wedding site

Henry James—not the American author but a millionaire exporter of lumber in the 19th century—built Overhills in 1897 as a wedding present to his son. Years later, when James's granddaughter needed a place to hold her wedding reception, her father simply expanded the ballroom portion of the house to include "the library," a room done all in teak, even the floor, which made it a perfect spot for dancing. Obviously, the mansion has weddings in its blood, but don't let that stop you from considering the place for other kinds of functions, for the house and grounds serve superbly in many capacities.

Situated at the top of a hill up a meandering drive, the white, three-story building backs up against a thick wooded area. Some 50 of the many trees you see were imported from all over the world by James. You can stage events on the stretch of lawn that lies between the house and the woods, on the covered octagonally shaped porch and its side veranda, or in one or all three rooms on the first floor.

From the front portico you enter a small vestibule and proceed directly to a center-of-the-house chamber that has shining wood floors, a black and white marble fireplace and a door in its octagonal bay wall that opens to the rear porch. To the right of this chamber is a bright room with white moldings and white-on-white period wallpaper, a tile floor, and French doors in an alcove leading again to the outside. To the left of the middle room is the ballroom, which is placed at an angle from the main house. The upper portion of the ballroom has wooden inlaid floors, white moldings, swag curtains, and another black and white marble fire-

73

place. The lower portion of the ballroom is paneled in teak with teak floors and French doors opening to the veranda.

CAPACITY

Reception: 200
Banquet: 200

Photo: Linda Johnson

LOCATION

From Baltimore, take I-95 south to Exit 47, and head towards Catonsville on Rt. 166. Stay right as you travel off the ramp and turn right onto South Rolling Road. Just before the first stoplight you'll see a large red church on your left; swing into the driveway and follow the lane around and up to the mansion.

FOOD/BEVERAGE

Overhills also houses the administrative offices of Whitehouse Caterers, Ltd., which handles all your catering and mansion rental needs. The caterer operates two kitchens, one on-site and the professional one nearby.

LIMITATIONS/RESTRICTIONS

Smoking is permitted on the front and rear porches, but not inside the mansion proper. Overhills is available anytime, year-round. To reserve a Saturday during the months of April through October, your guest list must number at least 100.

LEAD TIME FOR RESERVATIONS

Call a year in advance to reserve a date during the high wedding months: April through June, September and October. Otherwise, call for availability.

RATES

Weekday rental of first floor rooms: $35 per hour per room. Saturday rental of mansion and grounds: $800 for four hours, plus $200 for each additional hour. Friday or Sunday rental of the mansion and grounds: $500 for four hours, plus $175 for each additional hour. The site charges an extra $25 when you hold your wedding ceremony or reception outdoors. The nearby Rose Garden is available for weddings for $75. Catering rates start at approximately $20 per person for dinner and go up from there.

FACILITIES FOR THE PHYSICALLY HANDICAPPED?
YES NO SOME
X

THE RECTORY

24 West Saratoga Street
Baltimore, Maryland 21201
410/685-2886

A wholly exquisite old parsonage

From 1791 until 1986, this handsome, brick, late Georgian, early Federal-style house served as the residence for the rectors to Old St. Paul's Church, down the street. When the church's current rector opted to move his family to a more residential area, a historic architectural preservation organization stepped in to lease the place, restore it, and offer it for rent as a special event site. The parson's loss is your gain.

The first floor is the primary party area. Each of the four rooms reflects early 19th-century tastes in decor. Cheery, English, yellow-striped paper from the 1820s covers the walls of the wide entrance hall. The royal-blue shade of the library's satin drapes repeats itself in the room's medallion-printed carpet. Most of the furniture here and throughout the house is of the neoclassical or Empire period and was made in Baltimore during the 1820s and 1830s. Notice the 1815 "loo," or gaming table in the library, the scarlet square-back sofa in the parlor, and the 1815 marble-topped mahogany pier table in the dining room.

Up the winding stairway (framed so prettily within the arch of the entrance hall), is another grand central hall, a bridal lounge, and a formal board room. Outside is a brick courtyard and garden of seasonal plantings. Although The Rectory is located in the heart of downtown Baltimore, this spot is quite secluded.

CAPACITY

Reception: 100 inside, 175 inside and outside in the tented garden, 150 inside and out when you have a band and dancing

76

Banquet: 55 inside, scattered throughout the house; 100 outside, using a tent
Meeting: 25

LOCATION

On Saratoga Street, West, between Charles and Cathedral streets in downtown Baltimore.

FOOD/BEVERAGE

The Rectory prefers that you choose your caterer from its approved list. A large and fully equipped kitchen on the first floor offers two ovens, two refrigerators, a microwave, and a dishwasher.

LIMITATIONS/RESTRICTIONS

Bands, smoking, and dancing are permitted outside only. Chamber groups and piano music are allowed inside. Music outside must end by 11:00 P.M. Red wine is prohibited. You must rent The Rectory's tent if your party numbers more than 100 guests.

LEAD TIME FOR RESERVATIONS

The site accepts reservations up to a year in advance for weekend events. Call six months ahead for weekday parties.

RATES

The site charges $700 for a seven-hour event (allowing two hours for setup, four hours for the event, and one hour for cleanup), plus $100 for each additional hour. The 25-by-55-foot tent rents for $500 and is required for parties of more than 100 people.

FACILITIES FOR THE PHYSICALLY HANDICAPPED?
YES NO SOME
   X

The site has a ramp and restrooms that are accessible but not specially designed to accommodate wheelchairs.

ROLAND PARK COUNTRY SCHOOL

5204 Roland Avenue
Baltimore, Maryland 21210
410/323-5500

Entertain in Napoleon's nephew's summer home

You see, Baltimorean Betsy Patterson married Napoleon's brother, and it was their son, Jerome, who used the handsome stone house, now the school's administration building known as "Ward House," as his summer home. There are other interesting facts tied in with the school's history, just ask.

Certain first floor rooms in Ward House are available for private parties: the Cleveland Room (a sitting room), the foyer, the Lenci Room (a conference room), and a sun room opening to a brick patio. Exquisitely carved chestnut decks the walls of the Cleveland Room and the foyer. The Cleveland Room bends outward in a bay at the front, with windows overlooking the school's grounds. Antiques, Oriental art, a deep-green carpet, and comely, comfortable furniture embellish the small room. The Lenci Room is decorated in earth tones with more paneling upon the walls and swag curtains on the windows. The sun room is furnished as a casual lounging area. At the other end of the foyer from the sun room is the "link," so called because it connects Ward House with another school building. The link is all windowed walls and tile floor, a perfect area for dancing and the bar. The link also opens to the outdoor plaza, which can be tented to create more space for your function. Keep going along the link to the other building and you find yourself before the Harris Center, a kind of multi-purpose room that holds a large stage, tall white walls, and tile floor. The backdrop for the stage is a wall of windows capturing the school's front entrance and lawn in its sights. Like the link, this room allows parties to overflow to the front plaza

78

via double doors. You can rent the Ward House and Harris Center individually or together.

CAPACITY

Reception: 150 in summer, 125 in winter—using Ward House
Banquet: 165 in the Harris Center
Meeting: 20 in the Lenci Room, 300 in the Harris Center

LOCATION

On Roland Avenue, between Northern Parkway and Cold Spring Lane, in the northern outskirts of the city.

FOOD/BEVERAGE

You choose your own licensed caterer. A small kitchen is available in Ward House.

LIMITATIONS/RESTRICTIONS

The site is available daily for small meetings. Ward House is available Saturdays and after 2:00 P.M. Sundays for social functions. Harris Center is available Saturdays and after 2:00

P.M. *Sundays, subject to the school's own schedule. Smoking, music, and dancing are allowed. There is plenty of parking.*

LEAD TIME FOR RESERVATIONS

Call for availability.

RATES

Ward House: $700; Harris Center: $600; Ward House and Harris Center: $1,100. The school allows only one event a day and does not restrict your event to a certain number of hours.

FACILITIES FOR THE PHYSICALLY HANDICAPPED?
YES NO SOME
X

SHEPPARD PRATT CONFERENCE CENTER

6501 North Charles Street
Mailing address: P.O. Box 5503
Baltimore, Maryland 21285-5503
410/938-3900

State-of-the-art facility on hospital campus

Long known for its advances in the psychiatric and mental health field, the Sheppard and Enoch Pratt Hospital is fast gaining a reputation for its contributions in the conference center category. The institution built a spanking new, state-of-the-art facility in 1987 and invites outside groups whose missions are compatible with Sheppard Pratt's to make full use of it.

The conference center is encircled by 100 acres of peaceful and beautifully landscaped grounds. Inside are a 200-seat auditorium, a dining hall, five climate-controlled class-rooms, and attractive breakout foyers and covered outdoor balconies at either end of the building.

The overall style here is handsome practicality. The auditorium features tiered seats with adjustable writing surfaces, a rounded stage, and a full range of audiovisual services. Each classroom has large windows overlooking the picturesque grounds, wall-to-wall carpeting, movable desks and cushioned chairs, whiteboards, and audiovisual screens. Even the dining room is equipped with an audiovisual screen and microphone capacity. The conference center offers comfortable surroundings with no distractions.

CAPACITY

Meeting: from 20 to 70 in one conference room
Lecture/performance: 200 in the auditorium
Luncheon/dinner: 120 in the dining room

81

LOCATION

The conference center is located on the Towson campus of Sheppard Pratt Hospital, less than three miles from the Baltimore Beltway.

FOOD/BEVERAGE

The site has its own in-house catering service, but you may choose your own menu for your event. The site does not provide alcohol.

LIMITATIONS/RESTRICTIONS

The center is available to organizations that have a compatible mission with Sheppard Pratt's, and its rental is subject to the hospital's own schedule. Smoking is permitted only on the outside balconies. The site is best used as a conference space and for low-key receptions, dinners, and luncheons; it really isn't suitable as a wedding party place.

LEAD TIME FOR RESERVATIONS

Call at least one month in advance. Spring and fall are the heavy conference times of the year.

RATES

Auditorium: $350 for the whole day, $200 for a half-day's use. Classroom: $225 for the whole day, $125 for a half-day's use when your group numbers 40 or more people; $150 for the whole day, $100 for a half-day's use when your group numbers less than 40. Additional charges are for the use of audiovisual equipment, for example, $20 to rent the overhead projector and $70 to rent the VCR with television monitor; and for food service, which can range from $3.50 per person for breakfast to about $30 per person for dinner.

FACILITIES FOR THE PHYSICALLY HANDICAPPED?
YES NO SOME
X

SHIRLEY-MADISON INN

205 West Madison Street
Baltimore, Maryland 21201
410/728-6550

Victorian townhouse with a European touch

Pressed brick, 100-year-old marble pillars, Gothic stone carvings, terra cotta ornaments—if you delight in architectural details, you'll be happy just passing through the doors of the Shirley-Madison as your eyes sweep over these preliminary features. The first floor of the inn will only please you all the more.

Off the middle vestibule, dominated by a heavily carved, polished ash stairway spiralling up to the fifth floor, are the breakfast room, conservatory, and grand parlor. Mauve and blue are the favorite colors, antiques the preferred furnishings. Rooms have high ceilings and very long windows, fireplaces, and lots of woodwork. Despite its elegance, the inn feels rather homey. A courtyard in back provides another intimate setting, surrounded as it is by the inn's own walls. Overnight accommodations at the inn number 15 guest rooms and suites.

CAPACITY

Reception: 60 to 70 inside, 100 or so inside and in the courtyard
Banquet: 40
Overnight accommodations: 15 guest rooms

LOCATION

In the Mount Vernon district of Baltimore, a couple of blocks off of Maryland Avenue.

FOOD/BEVERAGE

You choose your own caterer, who may use the small kitchen located on the first floor.

LIMITATIONS/RESTRICTIONS

The inn is available for events any day of the year at any time. Events must end by 11:00 P.M. Smoking is allowed in designated areas. Rock groups are not permitted.

LEAD TIME FOR RESERVATIONS

Call three months ahead to reserve the inn.

RATES

$125 per hour, with a minimum of two hours required. The inn gives you a free hour to set up and another free hour to clean up your party.

FACILITIES FOR THE PHYSICALLY HANDICAPPED?
YES NO SOME
   X

SHRIVER-WEYBRIGHT AUDITORIUM

Historical Society of Carroll County Building
210 East Main Street
Westminster, Maryland 21157
410/848-6494

Hold your main event on Main Street

In beautiful downtown Westminster, amidst the antique shops and craft stores, you'll come across this Westminster mainstay. Here, Carroll County's Historical Society helps keep the past alive for visitors to and residents of the area and invites community members to make their own history on the premises. The building's Shriver-Weybright Auditorium, really more a hall or ballroom than an auditorium, is the site of many a Westminster wedding reception and business function.

A recessed entrance in the facade, separate from the entrance to the historical society's suite of offices, leads to a vestibule and then the event room itself. The hall has cream-colored walls, a parquet floor, six chandeliers, a piano, and windows viewing the back garden. Though the foundation of the townhouse dates from 1800, this part of the structure is just about 20 years old. Your party may flow to an outer room, when the society isn't showing an exhibit there, and outside to the small garden.

CAPACITY

Reception: 100
Banquet: 65
If you tent the garden, you may be able to accommodate more people.

LOCATION

From the Baltimore Beltway (I-695), take Exit 19 to I-795. Follow I-795 to Rt. 140 west, towards Westminster. In

Westminster, turn left on I-97 south and then right onto Main Street. Follow Main Street to 210.

FOOD/BEVERAGE

You may choose your own insured caterer. A full kitchen is available on the premises.

LIMITATIONS/RESTRICTIONS

Smoking and beer kegs are prohibited.

LEAD TIME FOR RESERVATIONS

Call anywhere from six to 12 months in advance.

RATES

The site charges a flat rate of $200, plus tax, plus $10 an hour for a security guard. Special rates are available for groups who want to hold four or more functions here a year.

FACILITIES FOR THE PHYSICALLY HANDICAPPED?
YES NO SOME
X

A ramp allows wheelchairs access into the building, but the restroom door is too narrow to accommodate wheelchairs.

THE STABLE AT MOUNT CLARE MANSION

Carroll Park

Baltimore, Maryland 21230

410/837-3262

At the edge of a park, down the hill from the mansion

Mount Clare, the mansion, was completed in 1760, making it Baltimore City's oldest residence. Here among their Hepplewhites and Chippendales and antique Chinese porcelain, barrister and Continental Congress member Charles Carroll and his wife, Margaret Tilghman, entertained George Washington and his ilk in their Georgian-style house. Tour the mansion and you'll learn more about the Carrolls and about life in the 18th and 19th centuries.

Mount Clare, the stable, is where your events come off. The brick building looks as old and untouched as the mansion up on the hill but actually suffered a fire at the end of the 19th century. Re-constructed in 1890 for the Mounted Police, the stable structure incorporates the cupola and other design elements from the original. You walk across a weathered old brick courtyard to enter the stable through large arched doorways that lead directly to the entrance foyer, a small but charming area with ceramic tile floors, brick walls, and bluish-gray painted woodwork. Straight ahead through glass double doors is another brick courtyard, this one enclosed on all sides by the stable's walls. This is the stable's most spacious spot. To either side of the foyer are separate halls that extend back. Sets of doors in these wings open to the courtyard, which may be tented.

CAPACITY

Reception: 200
Banquet: 100

LOCATION

From the Inner Harbor, proceed west on Lombard Street, turn left on Martin Luther King Jr. Boulevard, go two blocks and turn right onto Washington Boulevard. Go to the eighth traffic

light and turn into Carroll Park on the right. The stable is at the edge of the park, down the hill from the mansion.

FOOD/BEVERAGE

You're free to choose your own caterer. There is a kitchen on the premises equipped with an oven, refrigerator, dishwasher, sink, and counters. An auxiliary kitchen offers additional preparation space. The stable has 120 folding chairs and about nine rectangular tables that you may use.

LIMITATIONS/RESTRICTIONS

Events must end by 11:00 P.M. The site prefers that you smoke outside. The stable may be reserved for day or night functions year-round. Names of area musicians who play period music are available upon request.

RATES

The site charges a flat fee of $500 for weddings. Rates are negotiable for other kinds of events. A house tour costs $20.

FACILITIES FOR THE PHYSICALLY HANDICAPPED?
YES NO SOME
          X

The stable is accessible to wheelchairs via a ramp.

TUDOR HALL

Bel Air, Maryland 21014

410/838-0466

Birthplace of John Wilkes Booth

What? Wasn't John W. Booth the man who killed Abraham Lincoln?

One and the same. John Wilkes was born and raised here, as were eight of his siblings, including Edwin Booth, said to be one of the greatest Shakespearean actors of all time. Junius Brutus Booth, the boys' dad, had made a name for himself in England as a Shakespearean actor but moved to the United States in 1821 to start a new family. Tudor Hall was the elder Booth's dream house.

To get there, you travel down a gravel and dirt road that winds further and further into countryside until you come upon a well-kept lawn, a bevy of boxwoods, and the white brick cottage itself. Diamond-paned windows and a shaded front porch distinguish the exterior. Events take place outside on the lawn and inside on the first floor. There are wide-beamed floors and an open-hearth fireplace in the center hall. To the right is a library with floor-to-ceiling bookshelves filled with books on Booth family history, the Civil War, and the assassination. To the left is the music room, furnished with an 1863 Steinway piano and a bay window jutting out over the side lawn. Beyond the front hall is a living room and, beyond that, a dining room. Despite its name, Tudor Hall is really rather modest and down-home—and peaceful, thanks to its setting; intriguing, thanks to its history.

CAPACITY

Reception: 80 inside, up to 200 outside
Banquet: 50 inside, up to 200 outside with a tent

LOCATION

From the city, take I-95 north to Exit 80, Rt. 543, and follow it west as far as Rt. 22 (Churchville Road). Turn right onto Rt. 22 and follow the road to Tudor Lane, where you turn left. Follow

the lane back through the property posts until you reach the farm.

FOOD/BEVERAGE

You choose your own caterer.

LIMITATIONS/RESTRICTIONS

The site is available subject to the owner's own schedule.

LEAD TIME FOR RESERVATIONS

Call at least a month in advance.

RATES

The site charges $125 an hour, with a four-hour minimum and a $50 maintenance fee.

FACILITIES FOR THE PHYSICALLY HANDICAPPED?
YES NO SOME
      X

A ramp gains you access into the house. The restroom on the first floor can accommodate a wheelchair but isn't specially equipped with a grab bar.

THE U.S.F. *CONSTELLATION*

Constellation Dock
Baltimore, Maryland 21202
410/539-1797

The U.S. Navy's "Yankee Racehorse"

Dubbed the "Yankee Racehorse" by French sailors impressed with her performance during our quasi-war with France (1798-1801), the U.S.F. *Constellation* boasts a proud history. Launched in 1797, the *Constellation* is the oldest ship of the U.S. Navy and one of the original six frigates commissioned by the Continental Congress. Although she hadn't fired her 36 guns since Appomattox, the warship continued to sail until 1945. In 1955, the *Constellation* came home to rest in Baltimore, where she is moored now at a specially designed pier in the Inner Harbor.

If you've been anywhere near the Inner Harbor, you've probably seen her there. Maybe you've even boarded her for a closer inspection, in which case you know what a fascinating setting the *Constellation* makes for a celebration. As you explore the Spar Deck and the Gun Deck (the top and second decks), you have a chance to look at displays of uniforms, food, comfort items, guns, and equipment used on board during the 19th century and learn about ship life as the sailors would have lived it around the year 1861. To get an even better feel for the experience you can request tour guides, historic reenactments, and period music (sea songs and chanties).

You can rent the Visitors Center and the ship, or the second floor and terraces of the Visitors Center alone, but not the ship by itself. The Visitors Center is a modern complex connected to the *Constellation*; descriptive maritime displays are located throughout. Its second floor holds the Captain Thomas J. Murphy, Jr. Room, where blue carpeting, light wood paneling, an outside brick terrace, and great views of the harbor make this an attractive place to enjoy the food and drink portion of your event.

CAPACITY

Reception: 150 using the entire Visitors Center, 60 using the Captain Murphy Room and its terraces
Banquet: 55 in the Visitors Center, 36 using the Captain Murphy Room and its terraces

LOCATION

The U.S.F. Constellation is moored at the Inner Harbor between the Light Street Pavilion and the National Aquarium.

FOOD/BEVERAGE

You choose your own caterer. There is a workable kitchen off the Captain Murphy Room.

LIMITATIONS/RESTRICTIONS

The ship and Visitors Center are available for functions every day from 6:00 P.M. to 11:00 P.M. The Captain Murphy Room and terraces are available daily from 11:00 A.M. to 11:00 P.M. Only groups of 25 or fewer are eligible to reserve the Captain Murphy Room and terraces from 11:00 A.M. to 4:00 P.M.

LEAD TIME FOR RESERVATIONS

Call for availability.

RATES

You're asked for a donation of $1,250 to rent the Visitors Center and the ship from June 15 through September 14 and $750 to rent these two areas from September 15 through June 14; you're asked for a donation of $200 to rent the Captain Murphy Room and terraces during operating hours (groups of 25 or fewer only) and $500 to rent this area from 6:00 P.M. to 11:00 P.M.

FACILITIES FOR THE PHYSICALLY HANDICAPPED?
YES NO SOME
   X

Quiet Waters Park, Annapolis

Sites for 200 to 500 People

BALTIMORE MUSEUM OF INDUSTRY

1415 Key Highway
Baltimore, Maryland 21230
410/727-4808

Baltimore's roots revisited

A former oyster cannery on the Baltimore Harbor holds the secret to Baltimore's past as a giant during the Industrial Age, from 1830 to 1950. Working exhibits throughout the cavernous museum reveal the significant role that Baltimore played in shipbuilding, manufacturing, printing, food processing, broadcasting and communications, power generation, transportation, and sewing. Among the many facts you'll pick up when you launch an event here are these: Baltimore was home to the nation's first railroad, first power company, first industrial pressure cooker, first tin can, first gasoline-powered bus, and first packaged ice cream!

You can rent the whole space or a portion of it; in either case, staff will be on site to offer tours and demonstrations. Keep in mind that as a former factory, the place looks like a factory, with uncarpeted concrete floors and high ceilings with exposed infrastructure. The Radio Gallery and Truck Gallery are the two areas inside the museum where you may set up tables and chairs and music arrangements. The latter of these is the primary space, measuring 150 feet by 100 feet. A glass wall commands a view of the museum's deck; the pier, where docks the restored, 1906 steam-powered tug boat, the S.T. *Baltimore*; and beyond, the Inner Harbor. A sea plane prototype is under restoration inside the Truck Gallery. The deck and waterfront grounds may be rented separately from the rest of the museum.

CAPACITY

Reception: 500, throughout the museum; up to 300 using the deck and grounds alone
Banquet: 250, throughout the museum; up to 200 using the deck and grounds alone

LOCATION

From the Inner Harbor, go south on Light Street and turn left onto Key Highway; proceed three-fourths of a mile to the museum.

FOOD/BEVERAGE

The museum provides a list of recommended caterers, but you may choose one not on the list, subject to the museum's approval. The site provides preparation space and water hookups, but no kitchen. Tables and chairs are the caterer's or renter's responsibility.

LIMITATIONS/RESTRICTIONS

Smoking is prohibited inside the museum. Guests may wander through the galleries with drinks, but food must be kept to the Radio and Truck galleries or outside. Live music and dancing also are permitted in these designated areas. The museum is available for use weekdays between 5:00 P.M. and MIDNIGHT (except Wednesday evenings) and Saturday and Sunday from 5:00 P.M. until MIDNIGHT. Events are scheduled for a maximum of four hours.

LEAD TIME FOR RESERVATIONS

The site takes reservations as much as a year in advance, but call for availability.

RATES

Entire museum, including deck and waterfront area: $500 contribution.
Radio and Truck galleries and main exhibit areas: $350 contribution.
Deck and grounds: $150 contribution.
There is also a group admission charge of $2.00 per person, with a minimum charge of $100 for 50 people or fewer.

FACILITIES FOR THE PHYSICALLY HANDICAPPED?
YES NO SOME
X

BALTIMORE ROWING AND WATER RESOURCE CENTER

3301 Waterview Avenue
Baltimore, Maryland 21230
410/396-3838

Attractive boathouse on the Patapsco

Located just across the Patapsco River from the downtown area, the Baltimore Rowing and Water Resource Center grants you a view of the skyline that turns especially impressive at night when the lights of the city spark the sky. The red-roofed and brown-shingled stone building conveniently offers a wide deck off the back of its second level, from which you can gaze out at the river and boats or across the way to the complex of bridges and tall buildings that dot the harbor.

It's the second floor of the boathouse that you use for events. The main hall, which is the room that opens onto the deck, is the same width and length as the deck: 60 by 20 feet. This space sports a plain wood floor and teal-painted wainscoting trimmed with a reddish-orange border. Above the wainscoting, the walls are white and high, ascending to a pitched roof in the middle, with square skylights set in flat sections of the ceiling on either side of this peak. In the center of the back wall is a working fireplace. Down a corridor lined with glass cases displaying award trophys is the entrance and the other usable spot, the Resource Center, a smaller room with a tile floor and bay window looking towards the grounds and the water. The boathouse serves as the park headquarters for its surrounding 200 acres.

CAPACITY

Reception: 250 using the entire building, 150 in the main hall, 95 in the Resource Center
Banquet: 100 using the entire building, 72 in the main hall, 45 in the Resource Center

LOCATION

From the Inner Harbor, follow Light Street to Conway Street and turn right. Take Conway to I-395 and turn left. Follow signs to I-95 New York and stay on I-395 to your first exit, Exit 54. Exit 54 leads you to Hanover Street (Rt. 2) and across the Hanover Street Bridge. At your first right past the bridge, turn right onto Waterview Avenue. The facility is on the right.

FOOD/BEVERAGE

You are free to pick your own licensed and insured caterer. A good-sized kitchen is available, equipped with counter space, a sink, and refrigerator, but no stove.

LIMITATIONS/RESTRICTIONS

The center is available every day but Sunday, at any time. Events must end by 1:00 A.M.

LEAD TIME FOR RESERVATIONS

Call six months ahead to reserve the boathouse.

RATES

The rate for private, eight-hour (including setup, rental, and cleanup) functions is $600 on the weekends, $600 weekday evenings after 4:30 P.M., and $360 weekdays, from 8:30 A.M. to 4:30 P.M. There's also a charge of $15 if you use the fireplace in the main hall.

FACILITIES FOR THE PHYSICALLY HANDICAPPED?
YES NO SOME
X

THE BELVEDERE HOTEL

1 East Chase Street
Baltimore, Maryland 21202
410/332-1000

Baltimore landmark for nearly 100 years

You'll notice, as you flip through the rest of this book, that hotels are not included. Why The Belvedere Hotel, then? Well, in fact, The Belvedere is a hotel in name only now; new owners are turning the building into condominiums. But even if the Belvedere still operated as a hotel, the site would merit coverage in this book as a unique meeting place, for The Belvedere has been a cherished gathering spot for Baltimoreans and celebrated visitors since it opened its doors in 1903.

John Eager Howard built the Beaux Arts building on a low rise in what is now the downtown area and named it after his nearby estate, Belvidere, meaning "beautiful view." Rooms that once held party guests such as Mark Twain, Al Jolson, and Rudolph Valentino are the same ones you may use for events. On the lobby level is the John Eager Howard Room, with a marble-framed fireplace, paneled wainscoting, and a mural painted in 1936 depicting a younger view of Baltimore and the harbor. The same floor holds the Charles, a long hall with a high ceiling, and full-length, wide windows giving on to the street. On the twelfth floor are two formidable ballrooms, the Grand and the Assembly. The ceilings here are unbelievably high and in keeping with the overall dimensions of the extraordinary rooms. Both halls boast elaborate plaster work, and the Grand Ballroom also has an arcade that circles the perimeter. The famous 13th floor lounge has a nightclub feel to it and a pretty good view of the city. Note: At the time of this writing, the Belvedere was undergoing a renovation by its new owners and the specific decorative features of these rooms had yet to be installed.

CAPACITY

Reception: 400 in the Grand and in the Charles ballrooms, 250 in the Howard Room, 200 in the Assembly, and 150 in the 13th floor lounge
Banquet: 220 in the Grand, 200 in the Charles, 120 in the Assembly, and 160 in the Howard

LOCATION

At the southeast corner of Chase and Charles streets in downtown Baltimore.

FOOD/BEVERAGE

The site handles all the catering arrangements.

LIMITATIONS/RESTRICTIONS

The Belvedere's rooms are available all year at any time.

LEAD TIME FOR RESERVATIONS

Call a year in advance to schedule weddings, a month or so ahead for other events.

RATES

Call for rates.

FACILITIES FOR THE PHYSICALLY HANDICAPPED?
YES NO SOME
X

BOORDY VINEYARDS

12820 Long Green Pike
Hydes, Maryland 21082
410/592-5015

An old stone barn and great big fields

A stone's throw from Towson are the farms and rolling hills of an area known as Maryland Hunt Country. But these hills boast more than fine horses—they are also home to Maryland's largest and oldest vineyard, Boordy.

Boordy Vineyards is located on a picturesque 250-acre farm tended by the same family since 1936. As you approach the vineyards, you notice a fieldstone barn at the forefront of the grounds, framed against a background of lush farmland and fields. The large barn, built in 1830, houses the winery and serves as your party site. Two spots are available within the barn. The wine cellar, partly underground, has a low wooden ceiling, cement floor, and two-feet-thick stone walls; the cellar is available October 30 through March 15 of each year. The winery's second floor, which is available April 15 through August 15, is a single room measuring 50 feet by 80 feet. Thirty feet above you is the vaulted ceiling made of hand-hewn beams pegged in place. Add to this the thick stone walls, antique wine casks, a wooden floor, and a large wooden door that slides open to capture more light and a sight of the vineyards and countryside, and what you have is a very enchanting backdrop for a party.

CAPACITY

Reception: 80 to 90 in the wine cellar, 350 upstairs
Banquet: 50 in the wine cellar, 125 upstairs

LOCATION

From the Baltimore Beltway (I-695), take Exit 29 and turn left off the ramp onto Cromwell Bridge Road. Follow this road to the end and make a left onto Glen Arm Road. Go about three miles to Long Green Pike and turn left, then follow the pike two miles to the winery on the left.

FOOD/BEVERAGE

You choose your own caterer. (The winery can refer you to trusted area caterers and, if you want, will handle the catering arrangements for a fee.) By state law, the only alcoholic beverages that can be served on the premises are the wines produced here. A preparation area located next to the wine cellar has a microwave, a fridge, a sink, and counter space.

LIMITATIONS/RESTRICTIONS

Open flames and smoking are prohibited in the barn. If your party numbers more than 75 people, you'll have to rent a portable toilet for each additional group of 75. The vineyard is not available for special events during the harvest season, from August 15 through October 15. Otherwise you may rent the barn Monday through Saturday from 10:00 A.M. on and Sunday from 1:00 P.M. on.

LEAD TIME FOR RESERVATIONS

Call for availability.

RATES

The winery rents its barn for $500 during regular hours (Monday through Saturday 10:00 A.M. to 5:00 P.M., Sunday 1:00 P.M. to 5:00 P.M.). This rate covers a four-hour period. When the party takes place partly or entirely after hours, the vineyard charges as follows: three hours within regular hours/ one hour after 5:00 P.M.—$600; two hours within regular hours/two hours after 5:00 P.M.—$700; one hour within regular hours/three hours after 5:00 P.M.—$800; four hours after 5:00 P.M.—$900. Events lasting longer than four hours cost $50 for each additional half-hour. Tours are included in the rental of the barn.

FACILITIES FOR THE PHYSICALLY HANDICAPPED?
YES NO SOME
         X

BRICE HOUSE

42 East Street
Annapolis, Maryland 21401
Mailing address: International Masonry Institute
823 15th Street N.W.
Washington, D.C. 20005
202/261-1841 or 202/783-3908

Stately Georgian mansion in historic Annapolis

How appropriate that the International Masonry Institute uses the James Brice House as the headquarters for its International Masonry Center. The Brice House is a stunning example of bricklaying and construction craftsmanship, and, therefore, the ideal home for an organization devoted to the interests of union bricklayers, allied craftsmen, and mason contractors. Talented masons constructed the brick manor between the years 1766 and 1774; skilled union workers restored the Georgian structure to its original stateliness in 1983 and 1984.

Three rooms on the first floor and five rooms on the second floor, and the back garden, comprise the conference and party space. The rooms, at the time of this writing, were unfurnished—the better to show off the fine detailing of the moldings and mantles, and the easier for you to set up the tables and chairs required for your function. Wall and trim colors are true to the time when the house was built: robin's-egg-blue walls and pink ceiling in the ballroom, yellow-stained wall paneling in the sitting room, and again a light blue on the walls of the dining room. Upstairs chambers are equally colorful: pistachio green, peach and white, and gray-blue are a few of the shades found. Notice everywhere the high ceilings, old flooring, and painstakingly carved cornices. Doors in the ballroom lead out to the small but pleasant garden.

CAPACITY

*Reception: 150 inside, 250 using both the house and garden
Banquet: 80 inside, seated throughout the first floor rooms. This
number may be increased slightly if you use the garden.
Meeting: 30 to 40 in the ballroom, 12 to 15 people in each of
the five second-floor rooms*

LOCATION

*From the Baltimore Beltway, pick up I-97/Rt. 3 going towards
Annapolis. Stay on I-97 until you get to Rt. 50 east. Take Rt.
50 east to the Rowe Boulevard (Rt. 70) exit. Follow Rowe
Boulevard until it deadends at College Avenue and turn left.
Take College Avenue to King George Street and turn right.
Follow King George Street to East Street and turn right. The
house will be on your right.*

FOOD/BEVERAGE

*You must choose a union caterer. The International Masonry
Institute can recommend a few to you. There is a small but
modern kitchen on the premises.*

LIMITATIONS/RESTRICTIONS

*The house is available subject to the institute's own schedule of
commitments. Events must be in keeping with the dignified*

Photo: Lautman Photography

ambience of the site. Smoking is prohibited within the main building during standup receptions but allowed during meetings or other seated functions. Smoking is also permitted in the garden. Dancing and amplified music are not permitted. Flowers and decorations are allowed, but nothing may be attached to the walls or placed on period furniture. Red wine may not be served in the house.

LEAD TIME FOR RESERVATIONS

The house is sometimes available upon short notice; call for availability.

RATES

Conference use: $600 for the first floor, $400 for the second floor. These rates cover an eight-hour period.
Social functions: $500 for up to seven hours' use. Add $75 for each additional hour.

FACILITIES FOR THE PHYSICALLY HANDICAPPED?
YES NO SOME
X

CHEF'S EXPRESSIONS AT HUNT VALLEY

909 West Shawan Road
Hunt Valley, Maryland 21030
410/561-2433

Church and banquet hall all in one

If you have in mind a traditional banquet hall building when you set out for Chef's Expressions at Hunt Valley, you'll whiz right past the place on Shawan Road. Instead, look for a modern brick structure and the name "St. Mary's Orthodox Church," and you'll have no trouble finding it. On Sundays, the church serves as a place of worship for its congregation, on weekdays it operates as a day-care center, and at any other time, the hall is available as a meeting/party site.

Religious and day-care furnishings disappear when you have a function here. What remains is a wonderfully cheery, 4,000-square-foot hall with white walls and red wall-to-wall carpeting. There are arched lancet windows in one side wall, recessed lights, and a lobby decorated in shades of mauve-and-teal paisley. This is a site that's out to make things easy for you. When you rent the hall, Chef's Expressions offers you the use of a portable dance floor, cushioned chairs, and 72-inch round tables. Parking is abundant, too.

CAPACITY

Reception: 450
Banquet: 300

LOCATION

From the Baltimore Beltway (I-695), take I-83 west towards York, and exit at ramp 20B, Shawan Road West. Follow West Shawan Road to the church on your left.

109

FOOD/BEVERAGE

Chef's Expressions is also the name of the catering firm that leases the space from the church, so all your catering needs are taken care of by the firm. There is a full kitchen on-site.

LIMITATIONS/RESTRICTIONS

The building is available evenings Monday through Friday, all day Saturday, and after 2:00 P.M. on Sundays. Otherwise, there are no rental restrictions.

LEAD TIME FOR RESERVATIONS

The site takes reservations up to a year in advance and recommends that you call as early as possible to book weekend events.

RATES

A flat rate of $600 for weekend functions; rates for weeknight gatherings may be negotiable.

FACILITIES FOR THE PHYSICALLY HANDICAPPED?
YES NO SOME
X

CHESAPEAKE BAY MARITIME MUSEUM

Navy Point
(Mailing address: P.O. Box 636)
St. Michaels, Maryland 21663
410/745-2916

Eighteen acres on "great shellfish bay"

"Chesapeake" is the anglicized spelling of the Indian word "Chesepiook," meaning "great shellfish bay." Bet you didn't know that. There's plenty more you can learn at this 18-acre complex of 12 or so buildings that preserve and exhibit a vast selection of bay artifacts and highlight the history of the bay and its traditions in boat building, commercial fishing, yachting, waterfowling, and navigation. Alas, you won't be able to tour the exhibits during your event since the museum rents its two spaces, the Propulsion Building and the grounds, only after the place closes to the public. The lovely waterfront view never shuts down, though.

The Propulsion Building is a weathered-wood, barn-like structure designed to resemble a Baltimore steamboat terminal. One portion of the building will eventually house more than 50 steam and gasoline engines used in vehicles sailing the bay during the past two centuries. The other part is the party space: white walls, high ceiling, fresh-smelling wood beams. Great doors at the front of the building open onto the wide deck which wraps around to the side. From this deck you have a wonderful view of the Miles River and boats.

Those opting to rent the grounds likely will choose one of two spots: the area around the Tolchester Bandstand or the expanse of grass along the waterfront known as "Fogg's Landing." The bandstand is a large, white, octagonally shaped, Victorian gazebo, which was built in 1880 as an entertainment spot for musicians playing to summer vacationers. The museum allows you to tent the grounds at Fogg's Landing and near the bandstand.

CAPACITY

Reception: 175 in the Propulsion Building, upwards of 300 on the grounds
Banquet: 100 in the Propulsion Building, 300 on the tented grounds

LOCATION

From I-95, take Rt. 50 east towards the Bay Bridge. Stay on Rt. 50 after you cross the bridge and turn right on Rt. 322, the Easton Bypass. Follow Rt. 322 to Rt. 33 and turn right. Rt. 33 will take you straight into the town of St. Michaels, where you turn right at Mill Street and travel one block to the parking lot for the museum.

FOOD/BEVERAGE

You may choose your own caterer. A service kitchen in the Propulsion Building holds a refrigerator, stove, sink, and counter space.

LIMITATIONS/RESTRICTIONS

The Propulsion Building and grounds are available for private functions during the museum's off-hours, that is, daily after 4:00 P.M. October through December and after 5:00 P.M. May through September. Smoking is prohibited in all the museum buildings.

LEAD TIME FOR RESERVATIONS

May through the end of September is the museum's peak period, so call months in advance to schedule events during that time. Call weeks in advance to reserve the site during the off-season.

RATES

The same rate applies for rental of either the Propulsion Building or the grounds: $350 for up to 80 people, and $4.50 for each additional guest. You can rent both the Propulsion Building and the grounds and the charge is still $350 for up to 80 people, plus $4.50 for each additional person. These rates do not include the cost of the tent rental.

FACILITIES FOR THE PHYSICALLY HANDICAPPED?
YES NO SOME
X

ELKRIDGE-FURNACE INN

5741 Furnace Avenue

Elkridge, Maryland 21227

410/379-9336

Two old buildings joined together doth a glorious event site make

A Federal-style 1744 three-story tavern and its attached 1810 mansion for years were slowly going to the dogs. It was a disgrace, really, for the place is historic. The site was first charted in 1608 by John Smith of Pochahontas fame. Renowned Marylanders have called the estate home: Carrolls, Dorseys, and Ellicotts (of Ellicott City). An enterprising local caterer and the state of Maryland worked out a deal to save the site: the state owns the property and leases it to the caterer who has performed a remarkable restoration of the buildings. In early 1992, the caterer opened the estate as a combination inn, restaurant, and special-event location.

The 1810 house, originally a maze of masters and servants quarters, holds three dining areas on its first floor. Their very different but somehow complementary decors range from the front room's gray marbleized treatment of the window frames, the crown moldings, and the center ceiling medallion, to the middle chamber's gold-painted walls and flowered border, to the tavern-like back room with its greenish-gray wainscoting and an original, wonderful built-in cabinet extending floor-to-ceiling. A covered brick porch extends off the side of this room and leads to the spacious back lawn. On the second floor are three more dining rooms, one painted a mustard yellow and slate blue, another in shades of burgundy and wine, and the third all in yellow. Third floor rooms include a suite of breakfast, dressing, and bedrooms. The longleaf pine and fir floors are as old as the house, as is the tiger maple and walnut wraparound stairway.

The 1744 building was still in the process of being restored when this book was being researched, but plans were to place the inn guest rooms, a sitting room, and an overnight guests' restaurant/private party room in this portion of the inn, and to decorate throughout in an early American decor. Outside, centuries-old tall linden trees, hollies, rain trees, and various garden plots grace the 16 acres of grounds.

CAPACITY

Reception: 300 to 350 outdoors, 200 inside on two levels of the 1810 house, 125 on its first floor

Banquet: 50 in one room, 110 throughout the 1810 house
Eventual overnight accommodations: six bedrooms including one
suite, each with private bath

LOCATION

From I-95, pick up Rt. 195 east towards the airport. Exit at
Rt. 1 south headed in the direction of Elkridge. Once on Rt. 1,
you go to your first traffic light and turn left onto Levering
Avenue, which deadends almost immediately at Main Street.
Turn left onto Main Street, go half a block and turn right onto
Furnace Avenue. The inn is three-tenths of a mile down on
your left.

FOOD/BEVERAGE

The caterer who runs the inn caters all events held here, except,
possibly, those on Sundays, when you may bring in an outside
caterer. The inn may charge you if you do choose an outside
caterer for a Sunday function. There is a full catering kitchen on
site.

LIMITATIONS/RESTRICTIONS

The entire inn is available for special events all day, any day of
the week. The six dining rooms may be available on an
individual basis at any time. Dancing and music are allowed
inside the inn, but smoking is not.

LEAD TIME FOR RESERVATIONS

Call for availability.

RATES

Rates vary depending upon when you rent the inn and how
much space you use. For instance, you would pay $85 for
weekday use of the 1810 house's first floor rooms in January
through March of 1992 and as much as $400 for use of both
first and second floor rooms of the house on a weekend in April
through August of 1992. Use of the grounds will run you
another $200 on weekends, $100 on weekdays.

FACILITIES FOR THE PHYSICALLY HANDICAPPED?
YES NO SOME
    X

The site hopes to make its 1810 house first floor and restrooms
accessible to the wheelchair-bound by the end of 1992.

EVERGREEN HOUSE

4545 North Charles Street
Baltimore, Maryland 21210
410/516-0341

For "lovers of music, art, and beautiful things"

If you've ever wondered what the majestic yellow villa is that lies beyond the brick ramparts on the piece of property separating the campuses of Loyola and Notre Dame colleges on North Charles Street, you're about to find out. Evergreen is the name of the 26-acre estate and its glorious Italianate mansion. Owner and former ambassador to Italy, John W. Garrett, who had inherited the 1850 manor, bequeathed Evergreen to The Johns Hopkins University in 1942 and stipulated in his will that the house and its collections be shared with "lovers of music, art, and beautiful things."

So the estate is open to the public for tours, for cultural and educational programs, and for events. It's an amazing place. Among the rooms on the first floor of the main house are a drawing room with Vuillards, a Picasso, Rodins, and numerous other masterworks on the walls; a reading room and a library, both with book-lined walls containing Garrett's expansive rare book collection; and a bright yellow dining room decorated by Ballets Russes designer Leon Bakst. There are "beautiful things" everywhere, from the Tiffany wrought-iron gate at the house's front entrance, to the woodwork found throughout, to the mosaic floor in the central hall.

The two-story theater wing, separate from the main house, houses a gallery displaying Garrett's impressive collection of Oriental art and upstairs, the theater, whose every detail, from stage set to lamps, was designed by Bakst.

The 1870 brick carriage house is wonderful, too. Its long interior features a worn wood floor, paneled walls and ceil-

116

accommodate wheelchairs. The theater's entrance is one step up from the ground; restrooms on the first floor are handicapped accessible, and there is an elevator to take you to the second floor. The carriage house is at ground level, but its restrooms are not really accessible to wheelchairs.

GLASS PAVILION

The Johns Hopkins University, Levering Hall
3400 North Charles Street
Baltimore, Maryland 21218
410/338-8199

Thoroughly see-through

As transparent as a martini, the Glass Pavilion is a super place to tie the knot or have a ball, as long as you don't mind a few onlookers on the outside. In addition to its four glass walls, the large cube has a speckled, linoleum tile floor, a high, blocked concrete ceiling, and a modest stage area up three steps from the ground. A patio runs around the outside of the building, which lies at the back of the campus.

Another place to check out here: Shriver Hall. If you're in need of an auditorium, Hopkins's 1,118-seat hall is available, like the Glass Pavilion, during the summer. The Clipper Room on the second level of Shriver Hall is a multi-purpose space that may be used for lectures or receptions before or after a performance in the auditorium. One wall of the room is painted with a mural depicting tall ships sailing on the bay. The room also has a piano, windows overlooking the campus, and a door leading directly to the balcony of the auditorium.

CAPACITY

Reception: 450 in the pavilion, 200 in the Clipper Room
Banquet: 450 in the pavilion
Lecture: 450 in the pavilion, 1,118 in the auditorium, 200 in the Clipper Room
Performance: 1,118 in the auditorium

LOCATION

In mid-town Baltimore, on the Homewood campus of Johns Hopkins University, on the San Martin Drive side of the grounds.

120

FOOD/BEVERAGE

You may choose your own caterer or opt for the university's food service. There is no kitchen available in either the Glass Pavilion or Shriver Hall.

LIMITATIONS/RESTRICTIONS

The pavilion and Shriver Hall are available to outside groups from June 1 through the second week of August from 8:00 A.M. to MIDNIGHT weekdays and 8:00 A.M. to 1:00 A.M. Fridays and Saturdays. Smoking is allowed outside only.

LEAD TIME FOR RESERVATIONS

The university starts accepting reservations the first of the year for the coming year's calendar.

RATES

Glass Pavilion: $180 per hour; Shriver Auditorium: a flat fee of $2,000; Clipper Room: $65 per hour.

FACILITIES FOR THE PHYSICALLY HANDICAPPED?
YES NO SOME
X

THE GLASS VIEW

Bank Center Building
17th Floor
100 South Charles Street
Baltimore, Maryland 21201
410/536-3606

Observatory hidden in a high-rise

More than business is conducted in this bank building towering over the Baltimore downtown and Inner Harbor. Those who have ridden up to the seventeenth level know that this floor holds an excellent special event space. The Glass View is available year-round, any hour, for any type of function, from training sessions to wedding receptions.

Its corner-wall placement on the seventeenth floor gives The Glass View an interesting shape, as well as unbeatable exposure. The 2,351-square-foot space has walls of windows gazing out at such sights as the Baltimore skyline, the new stadium, the Inner Harbor, and the aquarium. The room is blue carpeted and furnished sparingly with antiques that once belonged to the founders of the building. A smaller room fronting Charles Street works as an intimate boardroom and is equipped with a conference table and chairs, and built-in bookshelves.

CAPACITY

Reception: 220
Banquet: 150, buffet-style; 120 for full sit-down service

LOCATION

A couple of blocks up from the Inner Harbor, at the corner of Pratt and Charles streets.

FOOD/BEVERAGE

The site uses its in-house catering service exclusively, except when the renter wants kosher catering. The caterer will customize the menu to suit your tastes. There's a small warming kitchen on the 17th floor and a large kitchen on the 3rd floor.

LIMITATIONS/RESTRICTIONS

You must be 21 or older to rent the site. The Glass View is available 365 days a year at any hour. Crab feasts are not permitted. Group parking rates may be negotiated with nearby underground parking garages.

LEAD TIME FOR RESERVATIONS

Call two months ahead for fall functions, one month ahead for all others.

RATES

Monday through Friday during the day you pay $300 for the use of the Glass View. Monday through Friday evenings, and Saturday and Sunday functions you pay $500.

FACILITIES FOR THE PHYSICALLY HANDICAPPED?
YES NO SOME
X

GOVERNOR CALVERT HOUSE AND CONFERENCE CENTER

58 State Circle

Annapolis, Maryland 21401

Annapolis: 410/263-2641, Baltimore: 410/269-0990

Maryland: 800/847-8882, FAX: 301/268-3813

Four styles under one roof

In the beginning, that is, the 1720s, Governor Calvert's house was a modest one-and-a-half story structure with a gambrel roof, just large enough for Maryland governor, Charles Calvert, and his family. Following a fire, the state of Maryland converted the remains into a two-story Georgian-style building, which served as barracks. Annapolis's mayor purchased the place in 1854, making it bigger and Victorian in style. In recent years, the Historic Inns of Annapolis Association restored the Governor Calvert House to integrate its different architectural elements while adding modern features.

In the end, what you have is a late 20th-century conference center residing in an 18th-century state house. The front rooms of the building are the oldest. Here, you may entertain in the central lobby, in the Blue Room, equipped with deep-set windows and French doors, and in the fascinating Hypocaust Room. The Governor installed the ancient heating system beneath the floor of this room to create a greenhouse effect for his citrus trees. A glass panel in the floor reveals the old hypocaust works. Windows in the Hypocaust Room overlook the side garden.

Beyond these three rooms are eight contemporary spaces. These include an atrium, a ballroom, three meeting rooms that can convert into bedroom/sitting rooms, the "Chinese Lobby," decorated in a Chinese motif, the Jonas Green room, a good spot for a banquet after you gather for cocktails in the garden, and a tiny boardroom bordering a back patio. Of these eight areas, the atrium is especially impressive.

The ceiling is three stories high; off to one side is a raised platform, perfect for the exchange of "I do's"; and a set of glass doors at the back leads to an enclosed and tented terrace.

The house holds 54 guest rooms, as well.

CAPACITY

Reception: from 20 in one of the meeting rooms to 500 using all available space
Banquet: from 12 in one of the meeting rooms to 320 using the atrium and ballroom, or 220 using the ballroom alone
Overnight accommodations: 54 guest rooms

LOCATION

From the Baltimore Beltway (I-695), take I-97 south towards Annapolis. Pick up Rt. 50 south and follow Rt. 50 to the Rowe Boulevard exit. Follow Rowe Boulevard, bearing right, to Church Circle. Follow the circle around to School Street and turn right. School Street takes you to State Circle and the Calvert House.

FOOD/BEVERAGE

The site handles all the catering arrangements.

Photo: Celia Pearson

LIMITATIONS/RESTRICTIONS

The Governor Calvert House is available every day, year-round for special events. Events must end at 11:00 P.M.

LEAD TIME FOR RESERVATIONS

Call a year ahead for weekend events, as soon as possible for weekday functions.

RATES

The site charges no room rental fees. Catering costs start at $13 a person for lunch and $20 a person for dinner.

FACILITIES FOR THE PHYSICALLY HANDICAPPED?
YES NO SOME
X

GREY ROCK MANSION

8901 Reisterstown Road
Pikesville, Maryland 21208
410/484-4554

An estate that combines a bit of the best from other mansions

Grey Rock Mansion's facade borrows from Mount Vernon in its display of columned portico; its foyer takes after an 18th-century English manor home, and the dining room is fashioned in the mode of a great chamber in a Philadelphia mansion once belonging to Benedict Arnold. The various styles and architectural features of the house blend winningly in a setting that is, above all else, a capital spot for entertaining.

Front rooms off the capacious entrance hall are the light-filled drawing room with pockets cut into its rear white walls so you can peek into the ballroom below, and the walnut paneled library, noteworthy for the intriguing antique carvings on the fireplace and the room's overall English-pub feel. Beyond the library is the formal dining room, featuring an over-large bay window. Across the hall is a generous landing and a curved stairway leading five steps down to the ballroom. This area is largest and offers a polished wood floor, brass chandeliers, and the same high ceiling found throughout the other rooms. Doors in a side wall take you out to the flagstone terrace, an expansive and shaded lawn, gardens, and a gazebo.

The Grey Rock property dates from 1698 and belonged to the John Eager Howard family until 1858; the core of the mansion is about 150 years old. A dairy/smokehouse and a tiny Howard cemetery plot still located on the estate are all that remain from the early days of the Howards.

CAPACITY

Reception: up to 175

129

Banquet: 150

If you use the patio and lawns, you can increase capacities for both a reception and a banquet to 225. Anytime you have more than 175 guests coming you must tent the patio.

LOCATION

Grey Rock Mansion is located a half-mile west of Exit 20 on the Baltimore Beltway (I-695).

FOOD/BEVERAGE

Valley Caterers of Worthington, the firm that manages the site, also caters all functions held here. The caterer prepares all kinds of food, ethnic or otherwise. There is a kitchen on the premises.

LIMITATIONS/RESTRICTIONS

Rock bands, confetti, and rice are not allowed. When your party numbers more than 175 guests, you must rent a tent for the patio. The mansion is available all day, any day, year-round.

LEAD TIME FOR RESERVATIONS

The site accepts reservations up to a year and a half in advance and recommends that you call that far ahead for weekend functions.

RATES

Weekends: $800. Note: A minimum of 100 guests is required to rent the mansion on a Saturday.
The site charges no rental fee for January, February, and Sunday evening events. Call for weekday and catering prices.

FACILITIES FOR THE PHYSICALLY HANDICAPPED?
YES NO SOME
           X

The restroom is accessible to someone in a wheelchair, but the easiest access into the house includes a step to the entrance.

INN AT HENDERSON'S WHARF

1000 Fell Street
Baltimore, Maryland 21231
1/800/522-2088

Charming waterfront retreat at Fells Point

Baltimore's Inner Harbor overflows with attractions and conveniences: Harborplace, the Convention Center, the National Aquarium, museums, and so on. But for some, the site's attractions might signify too much distraction, too much attention taken away from the business or pleasure that is the focus of your function. If you're looking for a city meeting place that is both favorably located yet not quite so in the thick of things, you might want to travel just a few minutes east to the quaint, 260-year-old neighborhood of Fells Point. Follow the cobblestoned Fell Street straight to the water, and there you will come upon the Inn at Henderson's Wharf.

The inn commands the first level of a six-story, 19th-century brick building that was originally a tobacco warehouse. (The other five stories house apartments.) The old brick walls are in evidence throughout the edifice, both in the inn's 38 guest rooms and in the public areas. Furnishings are just enchanting, combining period pieces with modern comforts. The inn offers the lobby, a courtyard atrium, a gallery, and two meeting rooms for private events.

Burnished cherry wood floors and paneling warm the lobby, whose decorations also include tapestry-fabric covered sofas and an overall deep green and dusty rose color scheme. French doors in the lobby open to the English garden courtyard, a long atrium of brick paved paths, fountains, seasonal plantings, and fancy wood patio tables and chairs protected by large white parasols. At the other end of the courtyard from the lobby is the gallery, where the vintage brick walls are hung with black and white photos of a younger Baltimore, the tile floor is set in herringbone pattern, and dim lighting and profuse green plants add appealing touches. The smaller of the two meeting rooms is the boardroom, which has a presentation wall, a mahogany table and swivel, floral-tapestry cushioned chairs. The main meeting room is equipped with an oak table and chairs

and a wall unit holding a white board, pulldown screen, tag board, and other business amenities. Each of the inn's 38 bedrooms looks out on either the courtyard or the wharf and is furnished in an English country tradition.

CAPACITY

Reception: 400 using the lobby, courtyard and gallery; 200 using the gallery alone
Banquet: 100 using both the courtyard and gallery, 80 in the gallery by itself, and 20 in the courtyard alone
Meeting: 12 in the boardroom, 40 in the main meeting room
Overnight accommodations: 38 guest rooms. Also available are 15 executive suites equipped with full kitchens, as well as larger, luxury, corporate apartments.

LOCATION

From the Inner Harbor, follow Pratt Street east to President Street and turn right. Take President Street to Fleet Street and turn left. Follow Fleet Street to Wolfe Street and turn right, and follow Wolfe Street until it deadends at Fell Street. The inn entrance is at the wharf end of the cobblestone street.

FOOD/BEVERAGE

You may choose your own caterer. A small kitchen and preparation area are available to caterers.

LIMITATIONS/RESTRICTIONS

The inn is a smoke-free building. Loud music is not allowed and events must end by MIDNIGHT. *The inn can accommodate dancing if you rent a dance floor. The inn is available for private functions year-round. The site recommends that you rent a tent when your party space includes the courtyard. You also can ask the inn to arrange a yacht charter for up to 80 people for meetings, receptions, or seated banquets.*

LEAD TIME FOR RESERVATIONS

Call four to six months ahead.

RATES

Gallery and courtyard: $600.
Board room: $150.

Main meeting room: $225.
The inn waives the rental fee when you book all 38 rooms and charges you a room rental fee on a sliding scale when you book some of the guest rooms.

FACILITIES FOR THE PHYSICALLY HANDICAPPED?
YES NO SOME
X

INN AT PERRY CABIN

308 Watkins Lane
St. Michaels, Maryland 21663
410/745-2200
1/800/722-2949
FAX: 410/745-3348

Preciousness personified on the Eastern Shore

When the occasion calls for royal treatment, the Inn at Perry Cabin is the first place you should explore. Situated on an expanse of brilliant green lawn fronting the Miles River, the inn offers an unbeatable view, service sublime, and an interior decor that's the perfect mix of comfort and elegance. Corporate executives have been pleased to find that the inn's special blend of pampering and privacy quite stimulates the old brain cells during business retreats; brides, likewise, delight in the sheer beauty of the site and in the staff's devoted attention to them and to every detail of their wedding celebration.

Sir Bernard Ashley, of the Laura Ashley decorating and fashion dynasty, is behind all this. Sir Bernard, who helped found the Laura Ashley business with his late wife Laura, spied the long white, Federal-style manor in 1989, purchased it, and refurbished it to his own specifications for a British country house. The inn, originally the private home of Commodore Oliver Perry's purser during the War of 1812, is now a showcase for Laura Ashley designs. Rooms are cozy but not cluttered and filled with antiques and reproduction furniture. All wallpapers and fabrics and most of the furnishings bear the Laura Ashley stamp.

Wedding receptions and other private parties generally take place in one or all three of the dining rooms. Each of the rooms opens through French doors onto the brick patio and from there to the lawn and water. Table linens, wall coverings, and drapes in two of the rooms are of a rose and jade floral design against a white background. The third room features dainty yellows and blues. The rooms interconnect but heavily curtained French doors can close off each of the rooms, one from another.

Additional public rooms used for business and other gatherings are the Mexican tile-floored conservatory, the snooker room (fully equipped with fax machine, overhead projector, and other office paraphernalia), and a suite of warmly inviting sitting rooms. Each bedroom is uniquely decorated. Croquet sets and bikes are available at the inn; staff can arrange other activities for you: fishing, boating, horseback riding, golf, and hot-air balloons.

CAPACITY

Reception: 100 to 125 inside, up to 300 outside
Banquet: 75 inside, 150 outside
Overnight accommodations: 41 guest rooms

LOCATION

From I-95, take Rt. 50 east to the Bay Bridge. Stay on Rt. 50 all the way to Rt. 322, the Easton Bypass, and turn right. Follow Rt. 322 to Rt. 33 and turn right. Rt. 33 will take you right into the town of St. Michaels. The Inn at Perry Cabin lies off of Rt. 33 (also Talbot Street) just past the center of town.

FOOD/BEVERAGE

The inn handles all your catering arrangements. Cakes are the one item that can be brought in from an outside caterer. The inn's cuisine has a French flair with a local influence.

LIMITATIONS/RESTRICTIONS

The availability of the inn for special events is subject to the inn's schedule of obligations to its overnight clientele. It's generally true that for large events taking place on weekends, you have to reserve the entire house, guest rooms and all. But do call for further information, since the inn considers each request on a case-by-case basis. Smoking is not permitted in the dining rooms.

LEAD TIME FOR RESERVATIONS

Call for availability.

RATES

Conference rates: from $250 to $300 per person per day. This rate covers bedroom accommodations, continental breakfast, lunch, afternoon tea, early morning coffee and mid-morning coffee break, meeting room and equipment use.
Party rates: call for these.
Overnight accommodations: from $195 to $450 per room per night.

FACILITIES FOR THE PHYSICALLY HANDICAPPED?
YES NO SOME
X

LEXINGTON MARKET

400 West Lexington Street
Baltimore, Maryland 21201
410/685-6169

The original farmers' market

Long before farmers started peddling their produce in parking lots or along suburban roads, there was Lexington Market. Started in 1803 as an open-air market, it simply grew and grew. In 1859, American essayist Oliver Wendell Holmes visited the food fair and was so amazed at the vast selection of gustatory delights that he dubbed Baltimore "the Gastronomic Capital of the Universe."

Except for a fire that kept the market closed for three years in the middle of this century, Lexington has remained in continuous operation since its birth. The market has changed a lot, of course. Today, Lexington Market is a sprawling, enclosed complex that houses the stalls of more than 130 merchants. When you hold an event here, you have a chance to review the whole scene. You can rent one or all three of the interconnecting Lexington Rooms, which are located on the second floor of the Arcade section of the market. These rooms are functional: the floor is white linoleum, the ceiling acoustic tile, the walls are white, and the lights are recessed. But a glass wall runs the length of each of these rooms, granting you an eyeful of Baltimoreans on the floor below as they banter and barter with the stall keepers and sample the various wares. The rooms, as well as the adjoining Arcade Balcony area, are also available after hours when the shops are closed and the crowds are gone. Quite frankly, though, the hustle and bustle of the marketplace is this site's main attraction.

CAPACITY

Reception: 130 in each of the Lexington rooms, or 385 throughout all three; 500 in the Arcade Balcony

Banquet: 105 in each of the Lexington rooms, or 305 throughout all three; 500 in the Arcade Balcony

LOCATION

On the west side of downtown Baltimore, between Eutaw and Greene streets.

FOOD/BEVERAGE

You can hire your own caterer, although the site prefers that you order your meal from one of the market vendors. There is a kitchen adjoining the Lexington rooms that has counter space, freezers, a refrigerator, and sinks.

LIMITATIONS/RESTRICTIONS

The Lexington rooms are available all day year-round. The Arcade Balcony is available for evening events only.

LEAD TIME FOR RESERVATIONS

Call for availability.

RATES

Daytime events in the Lexington rooms: $750 for up to 200 people, plus $2 for each additional person. Evening events in the Lexington rooms or on the Arcade Balcony: $850 for up to 200 people, plus $2 for each additional person. These rates cover a four-hour period—add $50 for each additional hour.

FACILITIES FOR THE PHYSICALLY HANDICAPPED?
YES NO SOME
X

MARYLAND HISTORICAL SOCIETY

201 West Monument Street
Baltimore, Maryland 21201
410/685-3750

Maryland's roots revealed

Settlers from Europe had already lived and prospered in the Maryland area for two centuries when a group of gentlemen in 1844 decided to found the Maryland Historical Society. In 200 years, Marylanders had made their mark in many fields, shipping, furniture-making, and politics among them. The men established the Maryland Historical Society to preserve the vast horde of treasures created and passed on by those first Marylanders.

Four spots in the museum are available for gatherings. The lobby is the first, an uncarpeted, fairly open area displaying handsome highboys, immense portraits of famous Marylanders, silver teasets, and assorted other antique objets d'art. Off to one side of the lobby, through a gallery devoted to ship model crafting, lies the boardroom. A heavenly meeting space, the boardroom is wood-paneled and has a vaulted octagonal ceiling, a long and wide elliptically shaped dark wood table surrounded by deep-seated green leather chairs, and built-in glass cabinets.

The Radcliffe Maritime Museum on the lower level is less glamorous but large and interesting. The exhibits do much to enlighten you about a 19th-century sailor's life, the kinds of vessels Maryland seamen have used over the years, and Maryland's four-century maritime history. Back on the first floor, there's an auditorium offering a stage, podium, blue-cushioned seats, two small balconies, and good acoustics.

CAPACITY

Reception: 200 in the lobby, 175 in the Maritime Museum, 375 using both the lobby and the Maritime Museum
Banquet: 135 in the Maritime Museum

Meeting: 25 in the boardroom
Lecture/performance: 354 in the auditorium

LOCATION

Just west of Mount Vernon Place in downtown Baltimore.

FOOD/BEVERAGE

The society has an approved list of caterers from which you must choose. A kitchen on site is equipped with three sinks, two refrigerators, a microwave oven, and a standard oven.

LIMITATIONS/RESTRICTIONS

Dancing, smoking, and cooking are prohibited. Seated banquets are allowed only in the Maritime Museum. The facility is never available for functions on Mondays and is available for Sunday rentals October through April. Otherwise, the auditorium and boardroom may be used Tuesday through Sunday at any hour, while the lobby and Maritime Museum are rentable after 5:00 P.M. Tuesday through Sunday.

LEAD TIME FOR RESERVATIONS

Call for availability.

RATES

Day rates: Rental charges are $100 per hour for the auditorium, $75 per hour for the boardroom and a flat fee of $75 for the use of the kitchen.
Evening rates: The museum charges $200 for each of the rental spots. In other words, it would cost you $800 an hour to rent all four locations, that is, the auditorium, boardroom, lobby, and Maritime Museum. The kitchen charge at night is a flat fee of $100 when there is no preparation work involved, $200 when there is preparation work involved.
In addition, there are charges for security, tables and chairs, table linens, and the services of building personnel.

FACILITIES FOR THE PHYSICALLY HANDICAPPED?
YES NO SOME
X

OAKLAND

5430 Vantage Point Road
Columbia, Maryland 21044
410/730-4801, FAX: 410/730-1823

A historic hall minutes from the mall

Oakland, or Oakland Manor, as people often call it, is a surprise to everyone who comes upon it. It's "Old World," while the rest of Columbia represents so much the new, modern world. Around the bend from a string of contemporary condominiums and minutes from Columbia's mall and town center, the mansion awaits you in silent grandeur.

Built in 1811, Oakland served as a country estate until the 1940s when it became, by turns, the property of a college, a nursing home, and a health spa, among other things. In 1986, the Columbia Association bought Oakland and renovated the structure to its current appealing appearance.

Through the front doors of the cream-colored Federalist-period building, you enter the spacious and radiant foyer. Proceed straight ahead and you're in the ballroom, another large and airy spot, with crystal chandeliers, yellow-toned walls and royal-blue curtains, and floor-to-ceiling windows and doors that open onto a wide, tiled veranda. Steps from the veranda, which can be enclosed, draw you down to the brick patio, the lovely landscaped lawn, and around to the side, the "Bishop's Garden." Retrace your steps inside the mansion and discover the first-floor library, complete with built-in bookshelves and leather chairs; the two second-floor conference rooms, identical in size (19 by 28 feet) and in color scheme (blue); and the lower-level meeting room and solarium. The second floor also houses the Maryland Museum of African Art, which may be opened for viewing during your event.

CAPACITY

Reception: 250, inside and out

Banquet: 250, when using the entire house, plus the outside; 150 when using the first floor rooms, plus the veranda

LOCATION

From the Baltimore Beltway (I-695), get on I-70 going west towards Frederick. Follow I-70 to Rt. 29 south to Rt. 175 west to your second stop light. Turn left on Vantage Point Road and turn right when you see the "Oakland" sign.

FOOD/BEVERAGE

You may choose your own caterer, as long as the caterer has a certificate of insurance, or you may ask Oakland to handle your food and beverage arrangements. The site has a serving pantry and a kitchen equipped with an ice machine, sink, refrigerator, hot box, and microwave.

LIMITATIONS/RESTRICTIONS

Smoking, red wine, red punch, and open flames or candles are prohibited. Music outdoors must be kept to a reasonable level. Oakland is air-conditioned. Rentals are for seven-hour periods, including two hours for setup.

LEAD TIME FOR RESERVATIONS

Oakland accepts reservations as much in advance as two to three years, but call for availability.

RATES

*Rates start at $750, but Oakland prefers that you call for
further information since prices can vary depending upon the
number in your party, the number of rooms you use, and your
area of residency and type of organization.*

FACILITIES FOR THE PHYSICALLY HANDICAPPED?
YES NO SOME
X

*Only the first floor, lower level, and restrooms are accessible to
someone in a wheelchair.*

GEORGE PEABODY LIBRARY OF THE JOHNS HOPKINS UNIVERSITY

17 East Mount Vernon Place
Baltimore, Maryland 21202
410/659-8197

An institute of high entertainment and higher learning

This superb building was constructed in 1875–1878 by George Peabody, a Massachusetts-born philanthropist. It operates today as it did then, as a free public library, although the institute is now a division of the Johns Hopkins University.

Two areas comprise the event-holding space: the outer Reading Room and the Main Stack Room. The Reading Room is comforting in its steadfastly traditional appearance. You may see the odd computer here, but mostly you'll notice the large old paintings and portraits hanging on the walls above the full wooden bookcases. There are long, heavy wooden tables with chairs, old manuscripts in glass cases, tall card catalogs (remember those?), and lanky windows staring out at Mount Vernon Place. Through wide wooden doors, you enter the Main Stack Room, the library's *piece de resistance*. Five tiers of bookcased stacks rise 56 feet above the marble open court to meet the skylight roof. Ornamental cast-iron and gilded balconies enclose each tier, winding all the way around the elliptically shaped chamber. The stacks on the court level form alcoves, which are furnished with more of those heavy wooden tables and chairs. The library maintains a general reference collection of more than 283,000 volumes on virtually every subject but music.

CAPACITY

Reception: 150 in the Reading Room, 400 using both the Reading and Stack rooms

Banquet: 230 in the Stack Room
Meeting: 100 in the Reading Room, 320 in the Stack Room

LOCATION

In the Mount Vernon section of downtown Baltimore.

FOOD/BEVERAGE

The university must approve both your choice of caterer and entertainment.

LIMITATIONS/RESTRICTIONS

The library may not be used for political functions. Smoking and open flames of any kind are not permitted in the library. Music must be kept to a reasonable volume. The library is available for rent Monday through Friday, from 3:00 P.M. to MIDNIGHT, Saturday from NOON to MIDNIGHT, and all day on Sunday.

LEAD TIME FOR RESERVATIONS

The library recommends that you call at least three months ahead to book your event.

RATES

Individuals and for-profit organizations: $2,000; nonprofit organizations: $800; off-peak (anytime January through March, July and August; Monday through Thursday evenings any month but December) rates for profit organizations: $1,500. In addition, there are cleaning fees: $75 for up to 125 guests, $125 for up to $200 guests, $175 for up to 300 guests, and $200 for more than 300 guests.

FACILITIES FOR THE PHYSICALLY HANDICAPPED?
YES NO SOME
       X

The entrance and restrooms are handicapped accessible.

PEALE MUSEUM

225 Holliday Street
Baltimore, Maryland 21202
410/396-1149 or 396-8395

"Oldest museum building in the country"

"Oldest museum building in the country," "first building constructed as a museum in the Western Hemisphere"—these appellations might lead you to expect a structure creaking with age and infirmities. But the Baltimore City Life Museums (BCLM), the city association that operates the Peale (and six other historic sites—see Baltimore City Life Museums, Museum Row Sites in the "Sites for 500 to 1,000 People" section and H.L. Mencken House in the "Sites for Fewer than 100 People" section) has taken pains to preserve the overall edifice while updating the interior.

American portrait painter Rembrandt Peale built the four-story Federal-style museum in 1814 to exhibit curiosities, things like mummies, stuffed birds, and a life-size wax figure of the fattest man in the world. In Peale's day, museums were more repositories of freakish objects than of fine art. These days, the museum features a history of and portraits by the artistic Peale family, changing exhibits on Baltimore's development, and collections of historical prints, photographs, and paintings. You may use three floors of the museum for events, although food and drink are restricted to the first floor. The galleries throughout are handsomely kept and include a marble-floored foyer and hallway leading to a rear chamber used for temporary exhibits, and a second-floor, pale green room furnished with a small semi-circular stage. There is also a brick courtyard filled with boxwoods and relief carvings and sculptures from the 19th and 20th centuries.

CAPACITY

Reception: 225 using both the museum and garden; 125 in the museum alone
Banquet: 24

LOCATION

At the corner of Lexington and Holliday streets, a few blocks north of the Inner Harbor.

FOOD/BEVERAGE

You may choose your own caterer, subject to the approval of the BCLM. There is a small kitchen holding a stove, refrigerator, and sink, just off of the offices area, which may be used for preparation space.

LIMITATIONS/RESTRICTIONS

The museum is available for events after 4:00 P.M. in winter and after 5:00 P.M. in summer. The BCLM gives its corporate members preference on the use of the facility for special functions. Food and drink must be kept to the first floor. Smoking is permitted outdoors only.

LEAD TIME FOR RESERVATIONS

Call at least a month in advance; however, events reserved more than six months ahead may be subject to re-scheduling when in conflict with BCLM programming.

RATES

$100 an hour on weekdays or $150 an hour Friday through Sunday, plus expenses for security, guides, the house manager, and setup and breakdown. User fees for corporate members vary according to their level of membership.

FACILITIES FOR THE PHYSICALLY HANDICAPPED?
YES NO SOME
      X

The restrooms are equipped to handle wheelchairs, but access into and around the museum is difficult.

PENNSYLVANIA STATION

1501 North Charles Street
Baltimore, Maryland 21201
202/906-2157

The perfect place to send off your party

Whether you want to throw yourself a farewell party, surprise a returning traveler with a welcome-home reception, or infuse a special occasion with a "going places" theme, Pennsylvania Station provides the ultimate site. The Beaux Arts-style train station, built in 1910, allows you to use its front entrance hall, that is, the section preceding the main concourse that leads to the train platform, for Saturday night functions.

The entrance hall is a two-story atrium whose ceiling is a series of three leaded stained-glass domes. The walls are cream-colored, the floor is made up of terrazzo, mosaic and marble, and magnificent doric columns punctuate the space. Off to one side are the station's trademark curved mahogany benches. As part of your contract with Amtrak, who owns the terminal, you must designate aisle ways through your event space to allow train passengers and their entourages access into and out of the station.

CAPACITY

Reception: 400
Banquet: 200

LOCATION

Pennsylvania Station lies a couple of miles north of the Inner Harbor between St. Paul and Charles streets.

FOOD/BEVERAGE

You're free to choose your own caterer. Catering is available through the in-station restaurant, if your prefer to go that route. There is no kitchen on the premises.

LIMITATIONS/RESTRICTIONS

The station is available for Saturday evening events only. Your event must be kept to the front entrance hall. Amtrak does require that you follow certain guidelines to allow their regular passengers easy access into and out of the station.

LEAD TIME FOR RESERVATIONS

Call at least six weeks in advance.

RATES

Amtrak charges you a flat fee of $1,000 for use of the station, plus any other charges to cover services provided for the event, such as on-site assistance and cleanup.

FACILITIES FOR THE PHYSICALLY HANDICAPPED?
YES NO SOME
X

PRESTON ROOM

25 West Preston Street
Baltimore, Maryland 21202
410/576-9298

Banquet hall housed in turn-of-the-century building

At one corner of West Preston Street and Maryland Avenue is the grand Greek Orthodox Cathedral of the Annunciation, founded in 1906. Facing the church on the other corner is a building of the same era, although not quite so impressive. It turns out that the Greek Orthodox Church actually owns this edifice and uses its first floor for offices. The church allows Martin's Caterers to manage and cater special events at the Preston Room, which occupies the second and third floors of the structure.

The Preston Room is basically a large banquet hall. Beige columns support the two-story room and the interior balcony that wraps completely around the top level. Some partyers like to ascend to the balcony to dance; others prefer to place an orchestra or string quartet here. The room's main level is carpeted on the perimeter, bare wood floor in the middle. Arched windows along the front and sides of the hall hint at the building's religious connections. Two huge glass chandeliers, as well as recessed lights and spotlights are positioned to illuminate your soiree.

CAPACITY

Reception: 450 to 500
Banquet: 220, with dancing

LOCATION

At the corner of Maryland Avenue and West Preston Street in downtown Baltimore, one street over from Pennsylvania Station. A brown marquee over the entrance announces "Preston Room."

FOOD/BEVERAGE

Martin's is the site's sole caterer. There is a kitchen on the second floor.

LIMITATIONS/RESTRICTIONS

The room is available all year-round, subject to the church's schedule. There are no other restrictions.

LEAD TIME FOR RESERVATIONS

Call at least one year in advance.

RATES

Rates vary from party to party. Martin's prefers that you call for this information.

FACILITIES FOR THE PHYSICALLY HANDICAPPED?
YES NO SOME
X

QUIET WATERS PARK

600 Quiet Waters Park Road
Annapolis, Maryland 21403
410/222-1777

Anne Arundel's prized park possession

With its three-story Victorian-style visitors center, Lutyens-like teak park benches, London street lights, and gourmet cafe, Quiet Waters is no ordinary county recreation area. Since it opened in September 1990, the 336-acre park has attracted more than 700,000 visitors, making it one of Anne Arundel's most popular spots.

Quiet Waters is fast becoming a favorite event site, as well. The facility offers six picnic pavilions and a meeting/reception space within a building called the Blue Heron Center. Two of the pavilions are 14-sided and fit 50 people; the other four are 18-sided and fit 100 people. Otherwise the pavilions share the same beguiling appearance: white-painted support beams, bare wood vaulted ceilings, concrete floors, extra-long wooden picnic tables, and secluded tree-shaded settings. A couple of the pavilions include a little playground area with wood swingsets and slides, and a couple of the pavilions are outfitted with large brick double fireplaces that split the space in two.

The Blue Heron Center is a white structure with a green roof and a rather modern design. The center houses the 54-foot by 53-foot Blue Heron Room, which has a high ceiling, windows along the sides and French doors leading to the brick patio and formal garden. Pink-trimmed woodwork and a blue-speckled taupe wall-to-wall carpet encircling a center tile floor are the room's decorative features. Wedding receptions and business meetings are equally suitable occasions to enjoy here. You may also choose any of the park's many scenic locations for a wedding ceremony involving no more than 50 guests.

CAPACITY

Reception: 225 in the Blue Heron Room, 50 in each of the two small pavilions, 100 in each of the larger pavilions
Banquet: 125 in the Blue Heron Room, 50 in each of the two small pavilions, 100 in each of the larger pavilions

LOCATION

From the Baltimore Beltway (I-695), take I-97 south to Rt. 50 east, to the Rt. 450 exit (Parole). Turn left at the end of the ramp onto Rt. 450 and then go right on Rt. 2 south (Solomons Island Road). Turn left at the light onto Forest Drive, go 3.2 miles to Hillsmere and turn right, and then quickly right again into the park.

FOOD/BEVERAGE

You may choose your own caterer or the on-premises restaurant to cater your event. The restaurant is flexible and will work with you to plan your menu. Keg beer is the only alcohol permitted in the pavilions. A beer permit is required to serve beer in the pavilions, and an alcoholic beverage permit is required to serve any type of alcohol in the Blue Heron Center. The Blue Heron Center holds a basic kitchen, but no cooking facilities.

LIMITATIONS/RESTRICTIONS

The pavilions are available from 9:00 A.M. to dusk year-round. The Blue Heron Center is available from 7:00 A.M. until MIDNIGHT year-round, except Christmas. Smoking is prohibited in the Blue Heron Center and amplified music is prohibited in the pavilions. Food and beverages may not be served outside the pavilions or Blue Heron Center. Tents are not allowed.

LEAD TIME FOR RESERVATIONS

The park starts booking reservations for the Blue Heron Center each July 1 for the following year. The park starts accepting reservations for the pavilions on January 1 of each year for the coming year and advises you to call as soon as you know your event date to get on the calendar.

RATES

Pavilion rates range from $40 for rental of one of the small pavilions by a school group during school hours to $300 for rental of one of the larger pavilions by a non-county group. Blue Heron Room rates are $100 for use of the room for two hours Monday through Thursday until MIDNIGHT, *Friday until 5:00* P.M., *with $50 charged for each additional hour; and $500 for use of the room for two hours Friday after 5:00* P.M., *Saturday and Sunday until* MIDNIGHT, *with $100 charged for each additional hour. Pavilion users must pay a per-car parking fee of $3 (county vehicle) or $6 (non-county vehicle). Blue Heron Center guests pay no parking fees. Keg beer and alcoholic beverage permits cost $50 and $75, respectively. Outdoor wedding ceremonies in the park cost $150.*

FACILITIES FOR THE PHYSICALLY HANDICAPPED?
YES NO SOME
X

SAINT JOHN'S COLLEGE

Annapolis, Maryland 21404

410/263-2371

Historic halls on a two-century-old campus

If you like a place with history, St. John's can't be beat. Four signers of the Declaration of Independence founded the college, many famous Americans were students here (including Francis Scott Key, who loved to ride a cow around campus), and during the Civil War the buildings served as a receiving station and barracks for Union troops who had been prisoners of the Confederacy and exchanged in the field for captured Confederates.

McDowell Hall, constructed in 1742, offers two rooms for rent. The Great Hall, where Lafayette once dined and danced, has white walls supporting a high ceiling and a railed balcony around its upper half. Other features include two chandeliers, portraits of past deans and presidents, and a platform stage. A classroom in McDowell makes a pleasant meeting space; it has long and wide wood tables, a bare wood floor, and windows looking out towards the central section of Annapolis.

Randall Hall is a London Georgian structure erected in 1903. Its Edgar T. Higgins Dining Hall is an example of neo-classic design with its white painted wooden columns, Palladian windows, and engraved cornices. A private dining room in the same building favors a Georgian period decor on a smaller scale.

The Francis Scott Key Building houses the orange-seated auditorium, adjoining tile-floored lobby, and a modern conference room called the "Conversation Room," which features two tiers of gray-cushioned chairs facing a long elliptically shaped table custom-made to fit the room.

The boathouse is another contemporary space. The large room on the second floor is the rental area. Here, glass walls and windows overlook College Creek and a pier and lead out to a small balcony. There's a bar, a dance floor area, and a piano.

Double and single dormitory rooms, which date from the late 1800s and early 1900s, are available during the summer.

CAPACITY

Reception: 250 in the Great Hall, 250 in the dining hall, 300 in the lobby and halls of the Francis Scott Key Building, and 200 in the boathouse

Banquet: 130 in the Great Hall, 175 in the dining hall, and 107 in the boathouse

Meeting/lecture: 160 in the Great Hall, 18 to 30 in McDowell Hall's classroom, 600 in the auditorium, 165 in the Conversation Room, and 200 in the boathouse

Overnight accommodations: 75 to 100 in the dorms

LOCATION

From the Baltimore Beltway (I-695), take I-97 south until you hit Rt. 50 going towards Annapolis. Follow Rt. 50 to the Rowe Boulevard (Rt. 70) exit and take that exit, traveling on the boulevard to the end. Take a left onto College Avenue, which leads you to St. John's on the left.

FOOD/BEVERAGE

The college requires that you use its on-site catering service for events in the dining hall and prefers that you use this service for events held elsewhere on campus, although it will consider outside caterers who are appropriately licensed and insured. There are two kitchens here, one in Randall Hall and a small one in the boathouse.

LIMITATIONS/RESTRICTIONS

The first thing you should know is that, generally, events held here must be in keeping with the academic purposes of the college. Further, the school's academic calendar and the students have priority over outside groups planning to schedule a function on campus. Smoking is not allowed in any of the buildings. Hard rock and loud music of any kind are prohibited on campus.

LEAD TIME FOR RESERVATIONS

Call at least two months in advance.

RATES

Rates vary—the college prefers that you call for this information.

**FACILITIES FOR THE PHYSICALLY HANDICAPPED?
YES NO SOME**
X

SAINT MARY'S SEMINARY AND UNIVERSITY

5400 Roland Avenue
Baltimore, Maryland 21210
410/323-3200, ext. 150

For those who receive the "calling" for a quiet meeting place

The Sulpician order of Roman Catholic priests who founded St. Mary's Seminary in 1791 may be looking on wide-eyed up in heaven as the seminary adds "conference center" and "special event site" to its list of functions within the Baltimore community. Those in command back on earth, though, offer this service with their blessing to interested organizations and individuals.

Part of the appeal of holding an event at St. Mary's Seminary and University is its situation upon 68 well-kept acres, whose pathways and gardens invite contemplative strolls. The site operates a first-floor suite of five meeting rooms and a lounge in a hushed section of the 65-year-old stone seminary/university building. The rooms each can accommodate different numbers of people, from six to 100, and are furnished in similar fashion, with gray carpets, cushioned or tablet-armed chairs, cream-colored tables, and all the necessary conference equipment: flip charts, pull-down screens, overhead projectors, and whiteboards. Down the hall is the lounge, a glass-enclosed room with comfy blue and red furniture.

The other space available is the school's dining hall, built in 1928 and renovated in 1989. The hall has that sort of prep-school feel, created, perhaps, by the stained oak wood paneling and pillars, high ceiling, stenciled walls, and chandeliers. This room may be used for luncheons, dinners, and meals associated with scheduled conferences, but not for wedding receptions.

CAPACITY

Conference: from 10 to 100 in the meeting rooms
Reception: up to 100 in the dining hall
Banquet: 250 to 300 in the dining hall

LOCATION

At the corner of Roland Avenue and Northern Parkway, on the northern outskirts of Baltimore City.

FOOD/BEVERAGE

The site's food service operation handles all your catering needs. When you have conferences here, you can opt to go through the cafeteria line at lunch time or choose a special menu for your participants, and you may eat either in the dining room or in the conference center.

LIMITATIONS/RESTRICTIONS

The conference center and dining hall are available all year-round, subject to the seminary's calendar. Smoking is permitted in the public areas but not in the dining hall or the meeting rooms. Dancing is not permitted. The site's primary users are nonprofit agencies, religious and educational groups, but others are welcome.

LEAD TIME FOR RESERVATIONS

Call three months ahead to reserve the dining hall, weeks in advance for the conference center.

RATES

*Smaller meeting rooms: $125 each; larger meeting room: $250. These rates entitle you to 9:00 A.M. to 5:00 P.M. use.
Groups connected to the archdiocese of Baltimore receive a 30 percent discount. There is no rental charge for the dining hall. Per person catering fees average $2.75 for breakfast, $5.50 for lunch, and $6.60 for dinner, when you choose items from the food service's daily menu. Special menus run about $7 to $10 per person for lunch and about $12 per person for dinner.*

FACILITIES FOR THE PHYSICALLY HANDICAPPED?
YES NO SOME
　　　　　　　X

Some parts of the facility are handicapped accessible, some are not; call for further information.

SAVAGE MILL

8600 Foundry Street
Savage, Maryland 20763
410/317-9286

Old textile mill takes on a new life

As a textile manufacturer, Savage Mill produced sails for clipper ships back in the 1820s, tents for Union and Confederate armies during the Civil War, backdrops for silent movies at the start of this century, and canvas for duffel bags and army cots throughout the two world wars. The mill served a variety of other purposes upon its closing at the end of the 1940s and now, in the last decade of the 20th century, it is coming into its own as an antique and retail center by day, party palace by night.

Savage Mill is actually a complex of six buildings, each named for the purpose it served when the place was a working textile mill ("The Cotton Shed," "The Spinning Building"), and now housing antiques, specialty, and artists' shops. Special events take place in the New Weave Building. Upon entering this building you descend a majestic double staircase to the main level. Mill shops line the sides and are closed but on view behind their glass facades during your event. The New Weave hall is big, and though the mill is old, the place sparkles with newness: shining, all natural hardwood floors and wainscoting; brightly white-painted pipes in the high wood ceiling; the glimmering clerestory windows holding 2,000 panes of glass.

Specialty and antique shops close each evening at 5:30, leaving the New Weave Room open exclusively for special events seven nights a week. You can take over the whole joint or confine your party to one spot. Smaller parties of 50 to 100 people may find the room they need for daytime functions in side areas of the hall. Mill owners provide you with linens, tables, chairs, and whatever else you need. There is also a brick courtyard at the mill's east entrance and a deck overlooking the original millrace.

CAPACITY

Reception: 400 to 500 using the whole building; smaller parties can be accommodated using a portion of this space
Banquet: 300

LOCATION

From I-95, you pick up Rt. 32 east (Exit 38A) and follow to Rt. 1 south, headed towards Savage/Laurel. At the first traffic light, turn right onto Howard Street and follow the street (it becomes Baltimore Street) until it deadends. At the deadend, turn left and go one block to Savage Mill; turn right into the parking lot.

FOOD/BEVERAGE

Baldwin's Restaurant caters all events held here. There is a kitchen on the premises.

LIMITATIONS/RESTRICTIONS

The New Weave Building is available for special events year-round, any day after 6:00 P.M. Smaller spaces are available during the day.

LEAD TIME FOR RESERVATIONS

Call for availability.

RATES

Rates range from $125 to $450, depending upon the number of people in your party and the amount of space you use. The site pro-rates fees for rental of the smaller areas. Rates cover a six-hour period. Call for more specific info.

FACILITIES FOR THE PHYSICALLY HANDICAPPED?
YES NO SOME
X

THE STUDIO
AT ART AND ARCHITECTURAL DESIGN

1112 St. Paul Street

Baltimore, Maryland 21202

410/837-1112 or 837-7549

FAX: 410/837-7548

A Gothic parish house full of surprises

Once the parish house for the splendid Christ Church, right next door, this Victorian Gothic structure has gone on to serve a more frolicsome purpose—parties, parties, parties. The architectural firm that owns The Studio has renovated the 120-year-old building, incorporating whimsical touches and inspired decorative details into the original design of first architect Bruce Price (father of Marjorie Merriweather Post and a prominent society architect). The result is a totally awesome but thoroughly fun setting for a celebration.

The Studio's main entrance is on Chase Street; you pass through the century-old cast-iron gates and proceed down a narrow brick-paved path to the building, which is set way back from the street. Straight ahead of you as you enter is the eight-foot-wide mahogany staircase with a grand archway overhead. To your left is the first floor's main hall, an open area with a stained maple floor, 16-foot-high ceiling, Gothic leaded windows, and white stucco walls. If you go right from the hall you enter a chamber that makes for a perfect bar and appetizers spot. The windows here are stained glass, the walls a periwinkle blue. Fey art pieces and modern light fixtures add an air of festivity to this ex-church room. Just outside this area is a finely landscaped garden including stone terraces, a fish pond, and a pergola with wooden walls.

Upstairs lies an even more audacious mingling of the sacred and the secular. A soaring cathedral ceiling of vaulted wooden beams tops the room 32 feet up. Windows are again Gothic and this time diamond-paned and leaded and surmounted with circular stained-glass panels. The oak floor is pickled and stained gray. A stand-alone loft at one end

gives you a closeup look at the ceiling and a vantage point for studying the action below. Beyond the loft is a separate suite of rooms that includes a lounge area and dressing room/luxury bath. At the other end of the hall is a gourmet kitchen with restaurant appliances, tiled red and black countertops, and a triple red sink. Off the kitchen is an adjunct bar/meeting area splashed in coral pinks and grays, with deepset windows overlooking the front walkway. There's more—but you'll just have to come see for yourself.

CAPACITY

Reception: 350, throughout; 250 in the downstairs hall, 40 in the downstairs side chamber, 150 in the upstairs hall, 40 in the coral pink room, 80 in the side lounge area
Banquet: 300 seated throughout; up to 170 in the downstairs hall, 30 in the downstairs side chamber, 60 in the upstairs hall, 20 in the coral pink room, and 30 in the side lounge area

LOCATION

At the northwest corner of St. Paul and Chase streets, right next to Christ Church, in downtown Baltimore. You enter on Chase Street.

FOOD/BEVERAGE

The Studio prefers that you choose a caterer from its list but will approve others who agree to abide by its regulations. Cooking on the premises is permitted in either the first or second floor kitchens. (Caterers need to supply their own portable stoves for use in the first floor kitchen.)

LIMITATIONS/RESTRICTIONS

The Studio is available 24 hours a day every day of the year. Smoking is permitted outside only. Red wine, cranberry juice, tomato juice, and sauces and hors d'oeuvres made with tomatoes are prohibited. The Studio will schedule two events for the same day, given that there is enough time between events to clean up and ready the site for the next function.

LEAD TIME FOR RESERVATIONS

Call as far in advance as possible, especially for weekend bookings.

RATES

Rates range from $550 for the use of one floor on a weekday in January, February, July or August to $1,100 for the use of the whole facility on a weekend September through December. These rates cover a seven-hour period; the site charges $100 for each additional hour, plus a $10 per-hour staff fee. For parties exceeding 200 people, the site adds on $2 for each additional person up to the 350 maximum.

FACILITIES FOR THE PHYSICALLY HANDICAPPED?
YES NO SOME
X

The Studio's entrance and first floor are accessible to those in wheelchairs. The restroom is wide enough but not specially equipped for wheelchairs.

UNION MILLS HOMESTEAD

3311 Littlestown Pike

Westminster, Maryland 21158

410/848-2288

In the same family since Washington's time

As Union Mills Homestead approaches its bicentennial in 1997, the site has cause for great celebration. The Homestead is a historic landmark, having served as a stopping place for both Union and Confederate troops on their way (on separate days) to the Battle of Gettysburg and for the likes of such American luminaries as Washington Irving and James Audubon. The gristmill is the oldest water-powered mill in the country to be operated continuously by the same family. In fact, the entire Union Mills complex, which includes the working mill, 23-room house-museum, a tannery, surrounding grounds, and miller's house, also has been maintained by the same family, the Shrivers, from the beginning.

Whatever cause you're celebrating, your function will come alive at this site. You may use the restored working mill, the tannery, and the grounds. Events in the old brick mill take place on its first and second floors, both of which are wide open rooms with many deep-set windows and displays of various mill artifacts.

The new hemlock tannery is immense, constructed like a tobacco barn with side walls that come down and flop over themselves on the outside, and with a crushed stone floor and high ceiling. Rustic. The grounds offer the picturesque Big Pipe Creek, which powers the mill, a charming foot bridge over the mill race, a goldfish/lily pond, and beautiful flower and herb gardens. You may arrange to tour the 11 open rooms of the museum while you're here to learn more about the history of the place and view original furnishings. At the very least, try out one of those old wooden rockers lined up on the house's shady veranda.

CAPACITY

Reception: 500 on the grounds or in the tannery, 160 inside the mill
Banquet: 200 on the grounds or in the tannery, 90 using both floors of the mill

LOCATION

From the Baltimore Beltway (I-695), take Rt. 26 west, to I-97 north, to Rt. 140 north, towards Gettysburg. Union Mills is located seven miles past Westminster on I-97 and 15 miles south of Gettysburg.

FOOD/BEVERAGE

You choose the caterer. The site has no kitchen. You or your caterer must provide the tables and chairs. You must obtain a license if you plan to sell alcohol.

Photo: M.E. Warren

LIMITATIONS/RESTRICTIONS

The grounds and tannery are available only in warm weather, the mill is rentable year-round. Events in the mill and tannery may run from 10:00 A.M. to MIDNIGHT; events on the grounds may run from 10:00 A.M. to dusk. Cleanup is your responsibility.

LEAD TIME FOR RESERVATIONS

The site often books weddings a year in advance. Call a month in advance for other types of events.

RATES

Entire site: $500; grounds, tannery, or mill: $200 each. These are per-day rates. During the winter, the site also charges you for the cost of heating the mill. The Homestead can rent you a 20-by-30-foot tent for $150.

FACILITIES FOR THE PHYSICALLY HANDICAPPED?
YES NO SOME
X

Restrooms and the tannery are at ground level and accessible to those in wheelchairs. The mill's entrance has two steps to overcome.

THE UNIVERSITY CLUB OF THE UNIVERSITY OF MARYLAND

419 West Redwood Street

Baltimore, Maryland 21201

410/328-CLUB

Coziness and convenience in a clubhouse

On the second floor of an otherwise unremarkable building in the heart of downtown Baltimore is this very club-like club. It's snug, it's got a kinder and gentler kind of style, it offers privacy and privilege. And to think that you don't have to be a member to rent it!

In all, there are five areas you can use. The least interesting but perhaps most functional spot is the banquet room, contemporary in feel, with peachy walls, pink-peachy carpet, recessed lights, acoustic-tile ceiling, and a piano. The banquet room can be divided by partitions into four smaller chambers.

The most popular space is the library, which people like because of its size—only about 12 folks can fit here—and its built-in bookcases, sturdy wood table, and small arched window overlooking Redwood Street. Next door is the parlor, good for stand-up receptions, and furnished with a fireplace, red leather couches, and mahogany paneling.

In the pub, there's a mahogany bar with green leather-cushioned stools, club chairs grouped around round tables, soft Irish-green banquettes lining the quail-colored walls, and windows viewing Paca Street. Adjoining the pub through French doors is the main dining room, whose features include unusual chandeliers, crescent-shaped windows, wallpaper splashed with a leafy, green tree design, and columned archways leading to alcoves. You can rent any one spot or the entire club.

174

CAPACITY

Reception: 250, using the four banquet rooms; 350, using the entire club
Banquet: 120, using the four banquet rooms; 250, using the entire club

LOCATION

In downtown Baltimore, a block down from Lexington Market and one street over from University Hospital.

FOOD/BEVERAGE

The club caters all functions but will work with the client to plan the menu.

LIMITATIONS/RESTRICTIONS

Members may use the entire club or any portion of the club whenever they want. Outside groups may use the banquet rooms anytime weekdays and the whole club anytime on the weekends. Smoking is permitted only in the bar.

LEAD TIME FOR RESERVATIONS

The club accepts reservations as much as a year in advance, but call for availability.

RATES

Rates are negotiable for any client, depending upon the space used. Call for further information.

FACILITIES FOR THE PHYSICALLY HANDICAPPED?
YES NO SOME
X

VALLEY COUNTRY CLUB

1512 Jeffers Road
Towson, Maryland 21204
Mailing address: P.O. Box 328
Riderwood, Maryland 21139
410/825-7110

A colonial style mansion of Southern hospitality

Here's a site that shuns banquet hall ambience and unabashedly proffers the personal approach. The mansion's very facade suggests a welcome, the way its pillared-covered porch sweeps out to greet you. The club's interior feels like the private home it once was: a profusion of mahogany woodwork, Oriental rugs, and parlor furnishings decorate first floor rooms. An area called the "clubside" is especially inviting: a paneled and brick working fireplace, wide, wraparound stairway, and dark mahogany wainscoting are some of its features.

The ballroom is the 130-year-old house's most modern addition. This 3,600-square-foot space has a parquet floor and a simple decor including wall sconces and a beigy-cream color scheme. Off the ballroom lies the sports bar, a cozy room whose walls are covered with clippings, photos, plaques, and other items commemorating Colt football team highlights when owner Art Donovan played for them.

CAPACITY

Reception: 350 throughout the first floor
Banquet: 180 in the ballroom, 210 using the ballroom and an adjoining space

LOCATION

From the Baltimore Beltway (I-695), take the Charles Street exit and turn right onto Bellona Avenue. Follow Bellona to Joppa

177

Road and turn right. Turn right onto Thornton Road, right again on Jeffers Road, and then left onto Templeton Road, which deadends into the club's parking lot.

FOOD/BEVERAGE

The site handles all the catering, which emphasizes Maryland and American cuisine. You may choose your own baker for wedding cakes.

LIMITATIONS/RESTRICTIONS

The site is available to members and nonmembers alike and may be used any day, any time of the year. Smoking is allowed.

LEAD TIME FOR RESERVATIONS

Call at least a year in advance for Saturday events in May, June, September, October, and December. Otherwise, call as soon as you have a date in mind.

RATES

The club charges no room rental fee. Catering costs average $45 per person for a sit-down dinner and four-hour open bar, excluding gratuity and sales tax. Call for more exact info.

FACILITIES FOR THE PHYSICALLY HANDICAPPED?
YES NO SOME
      X

VISTA ROOM AT TIMONIUM FAIRGROUNDS

2200 Block of York Road
Timonium, Maryland 21093
410/252-0200

A simple room with plain views

The Timonium Fairgrounds are home to more than the Maryland State Fair. As soon as the ten days of the fair end each Labor Day and the livestock return to their farms and the amusement rides travel to some other location, the Timonium Fairgrounds become once again a bunch of quiet buildings amidst gigantic parking lots. And for 355 days of the year, spirited activities of another sort take place in the Vista Room of the administration building.

The Vista Room is on the second floor of the administration building, which lies at the back of the fairgrounds. In spite of its name, quite honestly, your view is of the parking lot. The room itself, however, is tastefully appointed with a parquet floor, a bar at one end, mauve and grey furniture in a sitting area off to one side, and recessed lighting in the acoustic tile ceiling. A partition can divide the space into two. You can draw curtains over the expanse of window overlooking the parking lot, or not, as you desire.

CAPACITY

Reception: 300
Banquet: 300

LOCATION

From the Baltimore Beltway (I-695), take I-83 north to Exit 17. Go right off the ramp onto Padonia Road and follow the road to the second light, where you take a right onto York Road. Follow the signs to the Timonium Fairgrounds, and after you turn in through the gates, head towards the back of the grounds. The administration building is beside the Exhibition Hall.

179

FOOD/BEVERAGE

The site has a preferred caterers list but will consider your choice as long as the caterer meets Maryland state requirements. There is no kitchen here, just a preparation area.

LIMITATIONS/RESTRICTIONS

The Vista Room is available every day except during the ten days of the Maryland State Fair, which takes place on Labor Day and the preceding nine days. Bull and oyster roasts are not allowed.

LEAD TIME FOR RESERVATIONS

Call for availability.

RATES

$800 to $900. This rate guarantees you the room for as long as you want for one day. Chairs and round tables are included. Security fees are $12.50 per hour.

FACILITIES FOR THE PHYSICALLY HANDICAPPED?
YES NO SOME
X

WAVERLY

2335 Marriottsville Road
Marriottsville, Maryland 21104
410/313-5400

18th-century home restored for entertainment purposes

In earlier days, houses made perfect wedding presents, it seems. At least from father to son. (See the Overhills entry for another example.) In the case of Waverly, Revolutionary War hero and former Maryland governor John Eager Howard gave the white stucco building and its many hundreds of acres to his son George in 1811, when George married.

Today, the Howard County government owns the property, including the old house and the remaining 3.5 acres of grounds. Starting on the second floor, you have the use of the library, whose built-in book shelves contain many volumes that once belonged to the gov'ner, and a bedroom known as the "groom's room," since this is often the spot where husbands-to-be hide out before the ceremony.

The first floor holds a long entrance hall that runs straight from front to back of the house, the drawing room, dining room, "bride's room," and museum kitchen. Each of the rooms, upstairs and down, is furnished with antiques and the original floors—yellow pine everywhere but in the brick-laid kitchen. The wide lawns are good for tenting and are surrounded by wooded areas and shrubbery. You can hear the traffic on I-70, it's true, but you still feel far removed, thanks to the country setting.

CAPACITY

Reception: 500 outside, 150 in the house
Banquet: 300 outside on the tented grounds
Meeting/small luncheon: 15 in the museum kitchen

LOCATION

From the Baltimore Beltway (I-695), take I-70 west seven miles to Exit 83, Marriottsville. Go right off the exit about 1,000 feet to the entrance to Waverly on the right.

FOOD/BEVERAGE

You're free to choose your own licensed and insured caterer. The first floor contains a small but modern warmup kitchen.

LIMITATIONS/RESTRICTIONS

Dancing, smoking, and seated dinners are not permitted in the house. The museum kitchen is the only inside space where you may sit down together at a table, and that's only for small, daytime meetings, luncheons, or breakfasts. Otherwise, you may hold buffet meals in the house, with people seating themselves wherever they choose throughout the rooms. A tent is required on the grounds for sit-down meals. Waverly is available year-round, any day, any hour, but functions must end by midnight.

LEAD TIME FOR RESERVATIONS

Call at least six months to a year in advance for weekend events and as soon as possible for weekday functions.

RATES

Waverly charges a flat rate of $650 for use of the first floor, two upstairs rooms, and the grounds. The rental period is for a total of seven hours, which allows two hours for setup, four hours for entertaining, and one hour for cleanup. You must also pay a $200 security deposit, which Waverly will return to you after the event, if nothing is damaged. The museum kitchen rents for $65 for weekday meetings. Rates are scheduled to increase in 1992.

FACILITIES FOR THE PHYSICALLY HANDICAPPED?
YES NO SOME
   X

WESTMINSTER HALL AND BURYING GROUND

West Fayette and Greene Streets
Baltimore, Maryland 21201
410/328-2070

Dance on the graves of Baltimore's most distinguished

Everybody knows that Edgar Allan Poe is buried here, in Baltimore's oldest cemetery. But were you aware that this is also the final resting place for the city's first mayor, James Calhoun, a number of American Revolution and War of 1812 generals, and many others of the city's earliest crop of the best and the brightest?

Most of the tombs rest in the landscaped and fenced-in burying ground surrounding Westminster Hall, and you may amble among the gravestones when you have an event here. Some of the buried, however, lie in catacombs below the church. You can arrange for a tour of the catacombs and burying ground to top off your event.

Westminster Hall, completed in 1852, was built on brick piers above the tombs as a way to protect the graveyard without disturbing existing graves. The church has been restored, but its basic structure is original. What you see is a spacious hall—empty of pews or any religious paraphernalia—with shining floors and multi-colored stained-glass windows set in the side walls. A wide, gray-carpeted dais embraces the room on three sides. At the back of the hall, the ceiling arches above the restored 1882 pipe organ. Two good-sized balconies overlooking the hall at the front often are used for receiving lines and for small cocktail receptions prior to the sit-down dinner below.

CAPACITY

Reception: 250

183

Banquet: 200, when a cocktail party precedes the dinner; 250, when the event does not include a cocktail party
Lecture: 350

LOCATION

In downtown Baltimore, at the corner of West Fayette and Greene streets, and across from the Veterans Administration Hospital and University Hospital.

FOOD/BEVERAGE

You may choose your own licensed and insured caterer with the approval of the Westminster Preservation Trust, which manages the site. A service kitchen contains a commercial stove/warming oven, refrigerator, counter, and sink. The caterer or renter provides tables, chairs, and other items. Alcohol is allowed, but the sale of it requires a permit from the Liquor Board.

LIMITATIONS/RESTRICTIONS

Dancing must take place on the wood floor, not on the stage. Kegs of beer or soda are prohibited, as are rice, confetti, glitter, and flower petals. Events must end by 1:00 A.M.

LEAD TIME FOR RESERVATIONS

Call at least six months in advance.

RATES

Base fees for events lasting up to two hours and including up to 100 people are as follows: Monday through Thursday—$650; weekends and holiday season—$750. Fees cover the additional three to four hours required by the caterer to set up and clean up. Other fees include: $50 for each additional hour up to a total of five hours, and $75 per hour after that; $25 for each additional 25 people or fraction thereof; $100 for use of the kitchen; and $25 per hour per tour guide. Rates are subject to change without notice.

FACILITIES FOR THE PHYSICALLY HANDICAPPED?
YES NO SOME
X

WESTMINSTER RIDING CLUB

North Colonial Avenue
Westminster, Maryland 21157
410/857-5415 or 410/848-1244

A modern barn, but hold the horses

The Westminster Riding Club used to be—guess what—a riding club. In 1956, the horses departed, but the club remained, then a swimming pool was added, the barn renovated, and a new purpose founded. Today, the Westminster Riding Club is both a swimming country club for its members and a party site for whosoever desires.

Double doors in the large brown barn-like structure usher you in to the lower level foyer and then up a short set of steps to a long hall. French doors on one side open to a balcony overlooking the pool. A better view (if you're of the inclination) can be had at the back of the room, although for party purposes this area makes a good spot for a bar, with the aid of partitions to set it off.

Adjoining the first room is another long hall. This chamber has a three-part vaulted ceiling, windows on one side, and an alcove that suggests a place for the musicians to assemble. Recessed lighting, bare wood floors, and adornments of ivy plants and "points-of-light" lit branches hanging from the ceiling make this a cheery and contemporary kind of place to throw a party.

CAPACITY

Reception: 300
Banquet: 275

LOCATION

From the Baltimore Beltway (I-695), take Exit 19 to I-795. Follow I-795 to the end, where you pick up Rt. 140 west to Westminster. Once in Westminster, turn south (left) from Rt. 140 onto I-97, and turn right from I-97 onto Main Street.

185

Head two blocks along to North Colonial Avenue and turn right. The club lies at the end of this road on the left.

FOOD/BEVERAGE

You choose your own caterer. The club can offer you the use of its fully equipped kitchen.

LIMITATIONS/RESTRICTIONS

None.

LEAD TIME FOR RESERVATIONS

Call a year in advance for Saturday events, six months in advance for anything else.

RATES

Rates vary based on a number of factors, so the club says it's best if you call for more exact information.

FACILITIES FOR THE PHYSICALLY HANDICAPPED?
YES NO SOME
    X

Meeting: up to 50 in the conference room theater-style, 10 in the old kitchen

LOCATION

From Baltimore, take the Baltimore Beltway (I-695) to I-97 going south towards Annapolis. Follow I-97 to Rt. 50 towards Annapolis. Take the Rowe Boulevard (Rt. 70) exit and travel to the end of the boulevard and turn left onto College Avenue. Take College Avenue to King George Street and turn right; take King George to East Street and turn right; go a short ways and turn right onto Prince George Street. The Paca House will be on your right.

FOOD/BEVERAGE

You may choose your own licensed and insured caterer. A small but complete catering kitchen is available.

LIMITATIONS/RESTRICTIONS

The old kitchen and conference room are available anytime; the garden and terraces are available during the day for small functions, after 4:00 P.M. Monday through Sunday during the months of November through March, and after 5:00 P.M. Monday through Sunday during the months of April through October. Smoking is allowed only on the terraces. Drinks are allowed in the garden but not food. Food inside is allowed only in the ground-level rooms. Champagne, wines, and beer are the only forms of liquor allowed. The site permits small musical groups to play at low volume; music must end by 9:00 P.M.

LEAD TIME FOR RESERVATIONS

Call for availability.

RATES

Wedding ceremonies: $650; wedding ceremonies and/or receptions: $1,300 for up to 100 people, $1,800 for 100 to 250 people. These rates include walk-throughs of the house and garden. Call for rates for other types of functions. You must be a member of the Historic Annapolis Foundation to reserve the use of the site. (Membership is minimal; call for this information.)

FACILITIES FOR THE PHYSICALLY HANDICAPPED?
YES NO SOME
     X

The site has limited accessibility for those in wheelchairs, and the restrooms are definitely not accessible.

WORLD TRADE CENTER

401 East Pratt Street
Baltimore, Maryland 21202
410/333-4540

When the sky's the limit

Among the many buildings that dot the Inner Harbor's waterfront, one stands above the rest—literally. The World Trade Center is 30 stories high, with its 21st floor given over to two special event rooms and a boardroom. If a sweeping view of Baltimore's bay inlet figures in your party plans, consider this site.

The Maryland Room is the smaller spot, has fabric wall coverings, a mauve carpet, and windows along two long walls of the building panning the harbor and metropolitan Baltimore. Catty-corner to the Maryland is the Constellation Room. Here, the same floor-to-ceiling windows give you a more expansive view of the harbor that takes in the National Aquarium, the Maryland Science Center, bustling boat activity close up, and beyond to the bay. A marble dance floor and an adjoining bridal room are two other special features of the Constellation Room.

For those of you looking for a pleasant, out-of-the-office meeting space, the Governor's Room on this floor might suit the bill. In addition to the stellar overlook, the boardroom offers a glass-topped mahogany table surrounded by green leather swivel chairs, electronically controlled blinds, green carpeting, and audiovisual equipment.

CAPACITY

Reception: 370, using both rooms; 270 in the Constellation Room; 100 in the Maryland Room
Banquet: 305, using both rooms; 225 in the Constellation Room; 80 in the Maryland Room
Meeting/luncheon: 20, seated around the table; 26, using chairs on the periphery

191

LOCATION

At the Inner Harbor in Baltimore, right on Pratt Street.

FOOD/BEVERAGE

The site prefers that you choose a caterer from its list.

LIMITATIONS/RESTRICTIONS

The site is available year-round, anytime of the day. Smoking is discouraged. Red wine and grenadine are not allowed. Music is not permitted before 6:00 P.M. weekdays. The Constellation and Maryland rooms are adjacent but not connected.

LEAD TIME FOR RESERVATIONS

The site accepts reservations up to two years in advance.

RATES

Monday through Thursday, day or night: $900 (Constellation Room), $500 (Maryland Room).
Friday through Sunday, day: $1,000 (Constellation Room), $550 (Maryland Room); evenings: $1,200 (Constellation Room), $600 (Maryland Room).
Governor's Room: $300, anytime.
Each of these rates covers a five-hour period.

FACILITIES FOR THE PHYSICALLY HANDICAPPED?
YES NO SOME
X

Sites for 500 to 1,000 People

ANTRIM

30 Trevanion Road
Taneytown, Maryland 21787
410/756-6812

Country inn par excellence

Forty miles is no distance to travel at all when your destination is a place like Antrim. Antrim, which is named for the original owner's Irish birthplace, is an antebellum estate on 24 acres just a U-turn off of Taneytown's main street. Once a plantation manor, the 17-room, fired-brick inn has been renovated to a stunning fare-thee-well: its 1844 plaster moldings, soft heart pine floors, long windows, and marble mantels remain, while the owners have furnished the rooms with finely finished antiques, classic Schumacher wallcoverings, Oriental rugs, and artworks dating from the 17th and 18th centuries.

You may rent the entire inn, including the main floor, the guest rooms, the grounds, and the combination smokehouse/summer kitchen/slaves' kitchen, or a portion of the space available. When you reserve all of the first floor rooms, however, the inn recommends that you also reserve the bedrooms so as not to conflict with the inn's service to overnight guests.

On the main floor are two formal drawing rooms, an elegant dining room painted a lacquered cobalt blue, a library with leather couches and a modern media center, and a lovely veranda decorated with white wicker furniture and floral cushions. The veranda, which is covered by an awning, can be totally enclosed and heated in winter. The smokehouse/kitchen complex is a charmingly rustic spot with red brick floors, exposed beams, huge hearths, and arched doorways separating the three compartments one from another. Gravel paths, flower plots, and a pond embellish the landscaped lawns. The inn also offers a tennis court, tournament croquet, a par-three golf green, and a swimming pool.

CAPACITY

Reception: up to 600 on the lawn, 150 to 175 using the main floor of the mansion, 80 using the smokehouse
Banquet: up to 300 on the lawn, 60 in the smokehouse, 30 to 35 on the veranda
Overnight accommodations: 11 bedrooms, each with private bath, one honeymoon cottage with a fireplace and a jacuzzi, and one suite with sitting rooms, double porches, and a jacuzzi

LOCATION

From Baltimore, take the Baltimore Beltway (I-695) to Exit 19— I-795 north—to Rt. 140 west, going towards Westminster. Follow Rt. 140 west ten miles past Westminster straight into Taneytown. One mile into town, turn left (really a U-turn) onto Trevanion Road. The entrance to the inn is immediately on your right.

FOOD/BEVERAGE

Antrim handles all your catering and floral arrangements and works with you to plan just what you want.

LIMITATIONS/RESTRICTIONS

Sit-down functions inside the mansion are restricted to the veranda. Since the floors throughout are soft heart pine, women are requested to wear low heels, if possible. The inn is available as an event site year-round. If you reserve the entire first floor of the inn for a wedding reception, you're asked to book the upstairs bedrooms, as well, to ensure an exclusive "wedding retreat."

LEAD TIME FOR RESERVATIONS

Call at least six months in advance for large parties, four to five weeks ahead for smaller functions.

RATES

Overnight guests pay $125 to $225 a night Sunday through Thursday, $150 to $300 on Friday, Saturday, and holidays. The smokehouse structure costs $550 to reserve. To book the entire inn, including the main floor, garden, and smokehouse, you pay $1,500, plus the cost of overnight stays for each of the bedrooms. Call for other rates regarding the use of individual spaces, for instance, the garden alone, or the veranda alone.

FACILITIES FOR THE PHYSICALLY HANDICAPPED?
YES NO SOME
        X

Some parts of the inn are handicapped accessible, some are not; call for further information.

BALTIMORE CITY LIFE MUSEUMS, MUSEUM ROW SITES

800 East Lombard Street
Baltimore, Maryland 21202
410/396-3924 or 396-8395

Baltimore's past unmasked in a city block

The Baltimore City Life Museums (BCLM) association takes Baltimore's past personally — and invites you to do the same. In all, there are six museums and an urban park, each of which compels you to ponder what life was like for Baltimoreans in earlier days. The historic sites include the Peale Museum, H.L. Mencken House, Carroll Mansion, Center for Urban Archaeology, 1840 House, Courtyard Exhibition Center, and Brewers' Park. This entry deals with the latter five places, known as the Museum Row Sites, since they are clustered together within one city block. (The Mencken House has its own entry in the section entitled "Sites for Fewer than 100 People"; information about the Peale Museum appears in the section entitled "Sites for 200 to 500 People.")

The Carroll Mansion is a three-story brick townhouse that served as the winter home for Declaration of Independence signer, Charles Carroll of Carrollton. Furnishings and color schemes reflect the tastes of the early 19th-century upper class: eggshell-blue walls and butternut squash-colored trim, heavy drapes and canopy beds, elegant spiral staircases, and spacious hallways.

Next in the row is the Center for Urban Archaeology, a one-room exhibit that features a life-size excavation pit, and pieces of pottery and glassware from 18th- and 19th-century homes and businesses in the area. The self-guided exhibit allows you to play amateur archaeologist and decipher clues to unravel a picture of the past.

The 1840 House is the reconstructed rowhouse home of

wheelwright John Hutchinson and his family. You watch, and participate if you want, as staff act out everyday activities that would have taken place here in 1840, including cooking over the large hearth in the basement scullery.

Last in the block is the Courtyard Exhibition Center, a modern gallery space for changing exhibits that tell you something about the history of Baltimore, whether it traces the beginnings of black churches in the city or chronicles Baltimore's renaissance from the 1930s to the present. On the second floor is the "Education Room," which may be used for meetings.

These four spots are located together around a two-level brick courtyard, another available rental space. Across the street, but within the same block is Brewers' Park, a contemporary brick-paved plot on the site of an early American brewery. Brewers' Park, the courtyard and the four museums are available separately or together for functions.

CAPACITY

Reception: about 500, maximum, when you use the courtyard and all four surrounding museums. The individual capacities are: 125 in the Carroll Mansion, 75 in the 1840 House, 35 in the Center for Urban Archaeology, 100 in the Courtyard Exhibition Center gallery or 40 in the upstairs Education Room, and 400 in the courtyard.
Banquet: 35 in the Carroll Mansion, 20 in the 1840 House, 30 in the upstairs Education Room of the Courtyard Exhibition Center, and 125 in the courtyard
Concerts/picnic/performance: 300 in Brewers' Park

LOCATION

The Museum Row Sites of the Baltimore City Life Museums are located a couple of blocks east of the Inner Harbor, adjacent to the Jones Falls Expressway.

FOOD/BEVERAGE

You may choose your own caterer, subject to the approval of the BCLM. There are no kitchens on the premises.

LIMITATIONS/RESTRICTIONS

Except for the Courtyard Exhibition Center's Education Room, museum facilities are available for events after 4:00 P.M. in winter and after 5:00 P.M. in summer. BCLM corporate members receive preference on the use of the museums for special functions. Food and drink must be kept to the first floor of each site. Smoking is permitted outdoors only.

LEAD TIME FOR RESERVATIONS

At least a month in advance; reservations made more than six months ahead may be subject to change when BCLM programming takes precedence.

RATES

$100 an hour on weekdays or $150 an hour Friday through Sunday, plus expenses for security, guides, the house manager, and setup and breakdown. User fees for corporate members vary according to their level of membership.

FACILITIES FOR THE PHYSICALLY HANDICAPPED?
YES NO SOME
X

The Courtyard Exhibition Center, the Center for Urban Archaeology, the first floors of the Carroll Mansion and the 1840 House, and the courtyard are accessible to wheelchairs.

THE BALTIMORE MUSEUM OF ART

Art Museum Drive
Baltimore, Maryland 21218
410/396-6078

Magnificent space in Maryland's largest art museum

Neoclassical in design, the Baltimore Museum of Art is temple-like in atmosphere—not in the austere sense though, rather in its awesomeness. You get no better feeling for this than in the Fox and Schaefer Courts, at the heart of the museum.

The Fox Court is the original entrance hall to the 1929 building. Sixteen massive Greek columns, a 34-foot-high coffered ceiling, and a marble floor distinguish this long and elegant room. The museum's Modern and American art galleries lie to either side of the court.

Adjoining Fox Court through an arched entryway is Schaefer Court, a square atrium whose outer walls are lined with ancient Antioch mosaics and whose inner walls are actually a series of French doors and long Palladian windows revealing a central garden. This court, too, provides access to museum galleries, including the world-famous Cone Collection of early works by Matisse, Degas, Picasso, and other artists. The Fox and Schaefer Courts are available for events en suite or separately. The galleries housing the art may be opened during your event upon request.

In the museum's new wing is the Meyerhoff Auditorium, furnished with a stage and sound and projection equipment. Directly below the auditorium is the USF&G Court, a space of contemporary design that serves both as the entrance to the new wing and as a reception area for programs taking place in the auditorium.

199

CAPACITY

Reception: 1,000 (Fox and Schaefer Courts combined), 500 (Fox and Schaefer Courts each), 200 (USF&G Court)

Banquet: 520 (Fox and Schaefer Courts combined), 300 (Schaefer Court alone), 220 (Fox Court alone)
Performance/lecture: 363, in the auditorium

LOCATION

In the Wyman Park section of the city, just off of Charles Street. The museum lies next door to Johns Hopkins University.

FOOD/BEVERAGE

The museum provides a list of recommended caterers, who are familiar with museum policies.

LIMITATIONS/RESTRICTIONS

The museum's facilities are available daily, except Mondays, from 7:00 P.M. to 1:00 A.M. (Thursdays, 8:00 P.M. to 1:00 A.M.) The Meyerhoff Auditorium and USF&G Court can be made available during the day as well. The USF&G Court may be used only for stand-up receptions. Smoking, eating and drinking are prohibited in the galleries. Religious ceremonies are not permitted.

LEAD TIME FOR RESERVATIONS

Call three to six months in advance.

RATES

Fox and/or Schaefer Courts: Rates range from a $500 contribution for nonprofit organizations to a $3,000 contribution for private corporations and individuals. Members receive special rates. You should also know that the museum charges an additional per person rate, plus costs to cover security, supervision and maintenance expenses, which are estimated at $1,500 to $2,500.
Meyerhoff Auditorium: $500 for four hours, plus $100 for each additional hour. Rehearsal time, technical director services, and security (for this spot, count on spending $50 to $100 to cover security fees) are extras.
USF&G Court: $500, or $250, if used in conjunction with a program in the auditorium, plus security fees.

FACILITIES FOR THE PHYSICALLY HANDICAPPED?
YES NO SOME
X

COLLEGE OF NOTRE DAME OF MARYLAND

4701 North Charles Street
Baltimore, Maryland 21210
410/532-5314

Lovely uptown campus offers a multitude of meeting spaces

Notre Dame College has a space to meet any event planner's need: big and small, boardroom and classroom, formal and casual, great hall and cozy lounge. Impossible to describe them all, but here's a taste to get you going.

Fourier Formal Lounge: Fourier Hall's lounge area, once a library, is a paneled and carpeted room with a marble fireplace and living room arrangements of sofas, tables, and chairs.

Bryan Boardroom: On the second floor of the renovated 1873 Gibbons Hall is this room of high ceilings, long windows on three sides, and black and white photos of early graduates. The boardroom is suitable for meetings and luncheons. A kitchenette adjoins the room.

Marion Burk Knott Seminar Room: This is a contemporary spot, decorated in pale pinks and purples and furnished with comfortably upholstered chairs, a boardtable, and an electronically operated projection screen.

Doyle Formal Lounge: The same building that houses the dining hall offers this other large hall, with a wall of windows surveying the campus. Artwork hangs on the walls, otherwise, the room is empty of furnishings. The lounge is equipped with a piano and a sound system with microphone hookup.

LeClerc Auditorium: The college's most popular rental area has a lovely lobby, a stage, and seats 946, including the use of a balcony.

202

CAPACITY

Reception: from 20 in the Riley Room to 120 in the Doyle Formal Lounge
Assembly/lecture: from 120 in the larger classrooms to 946 in LeClerc Auditorium
Small lecture/performance: from 40 in the smaller classrooms to 240 in the Knott Auditorium
Meetings: Two boardrooms accommodate 20 to 30, the Marion Burk Knott Seminar Room and the Bryan Boardroom
Overnight accommodations: up to 350 in dorm rooms in the summer, depending upon availability

LOCATION

Notre Dame College is located north of the downtown area and south of Beltway (I-695) Exit 25, Charles Street.

FOOD/BEVERAGE

You must use the college's on-campus food service company. Kitchens and kitchenettes are scattered around the campus in different buildings.

LIMITATIONS/RESTRICTIONS

Campus facilities are intended primarily for the use of the college's students and for college-sponsored activities; the college rents space to outside groups when the space is not being used by the school and as long as the purpose of the group's event is in keeping with the school's mission. Smoking, dancing and music are allowed in designated areas. The college does not permit weddings or wedding receptions.

LEAD TIME FOR RESERVATIONS

Lounges may be reserved a year in advance. Classrooms and lecture halls may be reserved only a few months in advance, right before the beginning of each new semester.

RATES

Rates vary, from $100 to $800, depending upon the space reserved.

FACILITIES FOR THE PHYSICALLY HANDICAPPED?
YES NO SOME
      X

*Some of the spaces are handicapped accessible, some are not; call
for further information.*

THE ENGINEERING CENTER

11 West Mount Vernon Place
Baltimore, Maryland 21201-5190
410/539-6914

Lavish, sumptuous, sublime—a house superior in every way

It is easier to start with what the Engineering Society mansion does *not* have before attempting a catalogue of its many remarkable traits. The house does not come with acres of grounds. That's about it. The Engineers Club, as the place is sometimes called, is a townhouse in the middle of the city—no room for winding driveways, stately oaks, etc.

Nevertheless, the New York brownstone, Italian Renaissance-styled building manages to take up a lot of space. Created out of four smaller townhouses, the club comprises nearly 40 rooms spread over four levels and about half a city block. (It shares the block with the Walters Art Gallery—see that entry in the "Sites for More than 1,000 People" section.)

B&O Railroad president John W. Garrett gave one of the four townhouses to his son as a wedding present in 1872, and Robert and his wife, Mary Frick, spent the next 32 years expanding and remodeling their home. The Garretts were enormously wealthy and spared no expense, commissioning some of the best architects—Stanford White, John Russell Pope and Richard Morris Hunt—to design the residence.

On the first floor are five capacious rooms, including a theater, library, and drawing room. The lower level offers small dining/meeting rooms, the main dining room, and the bar. Two conference rooms on the second floor are also available. In addition, the mansion encircles a large, two-level brick and landscaped courtyard.

The large, two-story entrance hall features stained English oak paneling, a staircase spiraling under a great dome

205

of Tiffany glass, and a ceiling coffered in Moorish artistry. Louis XV is the main mode of the drawing room: gilded mirrors and furniture, gold drapes and a violet marble mantlepiece. Built-in bookcases and rich dark paneling line the walls of the English baronish library. The ballroom/theater has a stage, parquet floor, gold fabric-covered walls, and a coffered plaster ceiling of French design. The club's charms go on and on. If you're after grandeur, and you qualify to use the club, you may want to call and arrange a visit.

CAPACITY

Reception: 450 to 600, throughout the first floor
Banquet: 325 in the theater and adjoining gallery, 110 in the lower-level dining room, 15 to 40 in one of the lower-level private rooms
Meeting: 15 to 20 in one of the second floor boardrooms, about 35 in the other

LOCATION

The club overlooks Mount Vernon Place in downtown Baltimore.

FOOD/BEVERAGE

The club handles all your catering needs and works with you to plan your meal.

LIMITATIONS/RESTRICTIONS

The club is available solely to members, and only to those who have held membership in the club for at least a year. Although its charter does not limit membership to engineers, the club is required to maintain a balance so that at least 60 percent of its members are engineers. The club is available for special events all day Saturday and for "significant" special events on Sunday. The site also may be used for weekday evening functions, subject to the club's own calendar. Smoking is permitted in designated areas.

LEAD TIME FOR RESERVATIONS

Call well in advance to reserve the site—the club already has bookings for events ten years in advance.

RATES

The site prefers that you call for rental rates. Membership rates include a $500 initiation fee (waived for members of the armed forces wishing to join) and annual dues, which vary depending upon your particular status. For example, an individual under 32 pays $225 annually, an individual over 32 pays $350 annually, and a sustaining corporate member pays $600 annually. A one-time life-long membership is available for $3,000.

FACILITIES FOR THE PHYSICALLY HANDICAPPED?
YES NO SOME
   X

ENOCH PRATT FREE LIBRARY

400 Cathedral Street
Baltimore, Maryland 21201
410/396-5429

For a meeting of the minds or a lifting of the spirits

Toast your partner as you tease your intellect in the splendid main hall of Baltimore's central library. You don't have to be bookish to enjoy yourself here (though, admittedly, book lovers will feel in their element); the library's architectural and artistic features are bound to stimulate interest and conversation. Elegant in design, the library's soft lighting and strong character make this a classy yet unpretentious place to gather.

The hall is 100 feet long and lighted from the skylight ceiling, two stories overhead. Marble columns with ornate painted capitals support the structure, and windows from the second floor's offices look out onto the atrium. The library, built in 1933, salutes the heroes of printing and publishing. Murals at the north and south ends depict Gutenberg, the inventor of moveable type, and Caxton, the first English printer, while panels alongside the murals display the emblematic designs of early European publishers and printers. In addition, a frieze beneath the murals and panels bears the various insignia of 17 English and American printers, three Marylanders among them. Along the east and west walls hang six full-length portraits of Baltimore's own dynasty of colonial barons.

CAPACITY

Reception: 600
Banquet: 350

208

HARBOR CRUISES LIMITED

301 Light Street
Harborplace
Baltimore, Maryland 21202
410/727-3113

Rock your party on the water

Harbor Cruises Limited operates two large vessels that cruise the Chesapeake Bay while you feast, dance, and chat the time away. The *Bay Lady* is the larger of the two; the *Lady Baltimore* has a pointed, rather than a rounded bow; otherwise the two boats share the same basic design—and party formula.

Both the *Bay Lady* and *Lady Baltimore* have two enclosed decks and one open deck. Each deck holds a bar. The enclosed decks are carpeted, have tile dance floors and large windows running both sides of the vessels. In addition, the white boats with blue trim are air-conditioned and climate-controlled, have cushioned seats for their dining tables, and are decorated with hanging plants.

You can rent one deck, two decks, or an entire boat for any type of function. The vessels' usual cruise takes you on a 26-mile roundtrip that goes past the Francis Scott Key Bridge, Fort McHenry, the Aquarium, and other Baltimore landmarks. You can also charter the boat to take you to Annapolis, St. Michaels, or the C&O Canal.

CAPACITY

Reception: 600 on the Bay Lady, *500 on the* Lady Baltimore
Banquet: 400 on the Bay Lady, *375 on the* Lady Baltimore

LOCATION

You board the boats on the Light Street side of the Inner Harbor, down a ways from the Maryland Science Center.

FOOD/BEVERAGE

Harbor Cruises handles all your catering arrangements and will work with you to customize your meal. The food is prepared fresh on board in the galley.

LIMITATIONS/RESTRICTIONS

Smoking is permitted on the open decks only. You can reserve one or more of the enclosed decks or the entire boat, but not the open deck alone. Although the boats offer public cruises daily for lunch and dinner, moonlight cruises on Friday and Saturday evenings, and specialty cruises throughout the year, chartered events take precedence.

LEAD TIME FOR RESERVATIONS

Call for availability.

RATES

Rates start at $29.95 per person and go up from there. A minimum of 200 people is required to rent one deck of the Bay Lady; *a minimum of 175 people is required to rent one deck of the* Lady Baltimore. *Harbor Cruises may be flexible about this policy and may discount rates during the off-season.*

FACILITIES FOR THE PHYSICALLY HANDICAPPED?
YES NO SOME
X

MARYLAND ART PLACE

218 West Saratoga Street
Baltimore, Maryland 21201
410/962-8565

Regional art, modern building, urban setting

The Maryland Art Place had several locations before it finally settled in this three-story brick building in downtown Baltimore. The characteristics that make this a marvelous showcase for the works of regional artists are the same ones that endear it as a unique meeting place: a large L-shaped first floor, a light-filled second floor, high ceilings, bare white walls, and plenty of big windows looking out to the street.

Exhibits stay put and form the backdrop for your event. In all, you have 5,500 square feet to play around with, give or take a few feet, depending upon the amount of room taken up by a particular exhibit.

CAPACITY

Reception: 500 to 600, depending upon the space consumed by exhibits
Banquet: 100, using both floors

LOCATION

Between Howard and Park streets in downtown Baltimore.

FOOD/BEVERAGE

You may choose your own caterer, subject to the site's approval. A small kitchen offers a microwave, refrigerator, and sink for use.

LIMITATIONS/RESTRICTIONS

The site is available Monday through Saturday, from 6:00 P.M. to 1:00 A.M., and all day on Sunday. There is a three-hour

213

minimum required to reserve the place for an event. Parking is available in nearby parking garages and on the street.

LEAD TIME FOR RESERVATIONS

Call a month in advance.

RATES

Individuals and corporations: $200 per hour, with a three-hour minimum.
Nonprofit groups: $100 per hour, with a three-hour minimum. Add $50 to cover security costs for the first three hours, plus $10 for each additional hour.

FACILITIES FOR THE PHYSICALLY HANDICAPPED?
YES NO SOME
X

SCARLETT PLACE EVENTS

250 South President Street
Baltimore, Maryland 21202
410/962-8598

Two gracious ballrooms looking out to the harbor

"Elegance moderne" might be a good term to describe the style of these two ballrooms situated on the second floor of a rambling, multi-purpose new brick structure at the far east end of the Inner Harbor. The two rooms lie off a black and white marble-floored entrance and are of different sizes and decor.

The Plaza Room is smaller, measuring 3,340 square feet. Furnishings are vaguely art deco-ish in design: the carpet is a palette of grey, blue, pink, and white dashes, the drapes are luminescent grey sheers, and the wallpaper is a melange of gray and mauve. Big blocked windows on three sides overlook the Inner Harbor and downtown Baltimore.

The Scarlett Room is 6,775 square feet of party space, decorated in shades of rose and blue, with a floral carpet upon the floor and gold lead woodwork in the ceiling. Large windows and glass doors along a side wall behold the Inner Harbor while a wall of blocked mirrors at the back of the room reflect what's happening inside. Both this room and the Plaza offer an oak dance floor, an in-house sound system and podium, and direct access onto a brick and pebbled concrete terrace for better viewing of the harbor.

CAPACITY

Reception: 550 in the Scarlett, 225 in the Plaza
Banquet: 340 in the Scarlett, 150 in the Plaza

LOCATION

The Scarlett Place Building is located at the corner of President and Pratt streets, at the Fells Point end of the Inner Harbor.

215

The entrance to Scarlett Place Events is at President and Fawn streets, just off Christopher Columbus Plaza.

FOOD/BEVERAGE

Scarlett Place has an extensive list of approved caterers from which you can choose. The facility has a huge, fully equipped kitchen off the Scarlett Room.

LIMITATIONS/RESTRICTIONS

The site's only limitation is that parties must end by 1:00 A.M., since the building also houses condominiums.

LEAD TIME FOR RESERVATIONS

Call a year in advance to reserve a Friday or Saturday night in May, June, October, November, or December — the facility's most popular times. Otherwise, call anytime.

RATES

For those prime nights—Fridays and Saturdays in May, June, October through November—count on spending $1,100 for the Plaza and $1,800 for the Scarlett Room. Otherwise, rates for events vary, depending on the time of day, day of the week, length of time the room is reserved, number of guests, and so on. Scarlett Place grants discounts for parties held in January, February, July, and August.

FACILITIES FOR THE PHYSICALLY HANDICAPPED?
YES NO SOME
X

SPEAR CENTER BALLROOM

The Rouse Company Building
10275 Little Patuxent Parkway
Columbia, Maryland 21044
410/992-6555

By the shores of Lake Kittamaqundi

Find the dazzlingly white, avant-garde Rouse Company Building in downtown Columbia, take its elevator to the top floor (the fourth), and welcome to the Spear Center Ballroom.

First there's the lobby area. A sizeable space that adjoins two sides of the ballroom, it tapers into a plant-filled passageway overlooking an enclosed atrium at one end and widens, at the other end, into a comfortable gathering place with sofas and chairs scattered around and a wall of windows that offer views of Lake Kittamaqundi (a Piscataway Indian word meaning "friendly meeting place," appropriately enough) and the town plaza.

The immense ballroom can actually be cut to three different sizes, with the use of partitions. The unusual glass chandeliers and wood-slat ceiling, 30-by-30-foot hardwood dance floor, and brown wall-to-wall carpeting each contributes to the room's contemporary feel. Full-length glass doors line an entire wall of the ballroom, providing a panoramic view of the lake. Venture out. The outdoor, Z-brick terrace is perhaps the biggest draw here: The balcony wraps around the outside of the ballroom and allows you an unobstructed look at the peaceful lake and wooded area beyond.

CAPACITY

Reception: 600
Banquet: 600 without dancing, 400 with dancing
Meeting: 600, theater-style

LOCATION

*From the Baltimore Beltway (I-695), take I-70 west to Rt. 29
south, to Rt. 175 west. Rt. 175 is also Little Patuxent
Parkway. The Rouse Building lies at the end of the parkway on
the left.*

FOOD/BEVERAGE

*You may choose your own caterer. The kitchen here is any
caterer's dream, huge and modern and fully equipped with a
convection oven, two standard ovens, a warming oven, a
refrigerator, walk-in freezer, ice machine, and plenty of prep
space.*

LIMITATIONS/RESTRICTIONS

*Open flame candles are prohibited. Functions are usually kept to
four or five hours. The ballroom is available all day weekends,
and after 6:00 P.M. week nights.*

LEAD TIME FOR RESERVATIONS

*The center books up to two or three years in advance and is
especially popular in May as a prom site.*

RATES

*Prices range from $650 to $2,000, based on several factors,
including number of people in your party and the amount of
space required.*

FACILITIES FOR THE PHYSICALLY HANDICAPPED?
YES NO SOME
X

Sites for
More than 1,000
People

B&O RAILROAD MUSEUM

901 West Pratt Street
Baltimore, Maryland 21223
410/752-2463

Round up your friends in the roundhouse

It measures 240 feet across, 123 feet high, has 22 sides, and is 100 and some odd years old: that's the roundhouse at the B&O Railroad Museum.

Once a passenger car repair facility, the roundhouse now displays 22 of the oldest and most magnificently restored steam and diesel locomotives in America. Its mammoth dimensions and unusual exhibits make the roundhouse a spectacular place to entertain 2,400 of your closest friends!

In between meeting and greeting, dancing and eating, your guests will have a chance to peer at the rail cars surrounding them. Arranged like spokes in a wheel pointing towards the center, train car examples include a B&O sleeper car-caboose built in 1807; the first locomotive to run on rails, circa 1804; a mail car; and a heavy mountain handler built in the 1850s to transport people over the hard mountain grades of the Alleghenies. In the middle of the room is your dance floor, the original wooden roundtable once used to turn cars into the 22 repair bays. While you're here, you may also visit the back and front railyards full of other fine specimens of American railroad ingenuity, as well as the annex building, which contains train memorabilia and working model layouts.

CAPACITY

Reception: 2,400. Tenting will allow for even larger crowds. Banquet: 700 with dancing, 950 without dancing

LOCATION

The museum is located just one mile west of the Inner Harbor.

FOOD/BEVERAGE

You may choose your own caterer subject to the final approval of the museum. The museum offers caterers a preparation area with electrical hookups and a hose for running water, but not a full kitchen.

LIMITATIONS/RESTRICTIONS

The museum is available for special events everyday after 4:00 P.M. Events must end by MIDNIGHT. Smoking is prohibited within the museum annex building and in the Mount Clare Station building (where you enter) but is allowed everywhere in the roundhouse except on the wooden turntable. The museum provides off-street parking for 250 cars.

Photo: Larry Canner

LEAD TIME FOR RESERVATIONS

Reserve at least one month in advance.

RATES

The museum charges $2,100 for the first 200 guests, plus $6 for each additional guest.

FACILITIES FOR THE PHYSICALLY HANDICAPPED?
YES NO SOME
X

THE BALTIMORE GRAND

401 West Fayette Street
Baltimore, Maryland 21201
410/727-5678
FAX: 410/727-5689

Banks into ballrooms

At the turn of the century, a large belle nouveau-style building was erected on this spot, and two banks conducted their business here. In the 1980s, a massive renovation turned the banks into ballrooms, and the structure took on a new life as a favorite city party site, The Baltimore Grand.

What were once the main lobbies of the banks are now the Chesapeake and Loyola Ballrooms. The Chesapeake is the larger of the two, measuring about 56 feet by 110 feet and boasting a 55-foot-high ceiling. Traces of the bank's original decor—the unusable but decorative balcony and the Tiffany stained-glass green crescents below the ceiling—add precious touches to this modern space. The room is fully carpeted and has walls of attractive acoustical paneling that are topped with hand-crafted plaster work.

Next door, the Loyola Ballroom measures nearly 43 feet by 84 feet. The room's smaller proportions, champagne-tinted brocade wallpaper, and two crystal and gilded chandeliers hanging from an 18-foot-high ceiling make this a rather more intimate area than the Chesapeake.

For business meetings, VIP luncheons and the like, look to the prized H.L. Mencken Boardroom. The room is exquisitely appointed with a parquet floor, mahogany-paneled walls, the original ornamental plaster ceiling, and an Italian marble fireplace. Forty-eight is about the maximum the room can accommodate.

The Baltimore Grand has a grand lobby, too, which may be used as supplemental space for your event. The building is attached to a parking garage with 1,000 spaces available for pre-validation.

CAPACITY

Reception: 1,200, using both ballrooms; 540 using only the Chesapeake; 360 using only the Loyola; 50, using the Mencken Room
Banquet: 1,000, using both ballrooms and the lobby; 480, using only the Chesapeake; 270, using only the Loyola. If you use both the Chesapeake and Loyola ballrooms and set up bars and a dance area, the rooms can accommodate a maximum of 600 comfortably.
Small dinner/luncheon/meeting: from 20 to 48 (depending on seating arrangements), in the Mencken Room

LOCATION

In downtown Baltimore, between West Paca and Eutaw streets.

FOOD/BEVERAGE

The Baltimore Grand has its own in-house catering service, The Grand Caterer, which caters all but kosher events. The site can provide a kosher kitchen and a list of approved kosher caterers.

LIMITATIONS/RESTRICTIONS

The site is available all year-round. There are no real restrictions here, but discuss your requirements with the site manager.

LEAD TIME FOR RESERVATIONS

The site takes reservations a year in advance, but call for availability.

RATES

Rates are variable, depending upon the day, time, season, and space reserved for the event. Rates can range from $150 for a luncheon in the Mencken Room to $4,200 for the use of the whole facility.

FACILITIES FOR THE PHYSICALLY HANDICAPPED?
YES NO SOME
X

THE BALTIMORE ZOO

Druid Hill Park
Baltimore, Maryland 21217
410/396-6165 or 396-7102

Help preserve wildlife — throw a party at the zoo

You can say "boo" to the Siberian tigers, make faces at the monkeys, and imitate the penguins' walk and no one will look askance, even if you do have a glass of champagne in your hand. Hey, this is the zoo, a place that sanctions, almost demands uninhibited behavior. So if you're having a party here, get ready to loosen that tie, let your hair down and cavort among the animals.

You can rent the entire zoo, an area called the Village Green or tented portions of the Green, the Polar Bear Square Tent, the Waterfowl Lake Pavilion and grounds, or the Mansion House porch.

The most civilized setting, if that's what you want, is the Mansion House porch. Built in 1801 as a residence for the Rogers family, the Mansion House now holds the zoo's administrative offices. The 20-foot-wide porch encircling the large square building has a high, gray-painted wood ceiling, sand-colored carpeting, and a view of the zoo.

The Waterfowl Lake Pavilion sits amidst wide grassy slopes adjacent to the scenic Waterfowl Lake. The lawn is dotted with trees and picnic tables and there are swingsets for the kiddies. The Village Green includes two tented, concrete-floored squares with picnic tables, and the adjoining Children's Zoo. The Polar Bear Square Tent is also a covered, paved square furnished with picnic tables.

CAPACITY

Reception: thousands throughout the zoo, up to 5,000 on the Waterfowl Lake Pavilion grounds, 600 on the Mansion House porch, 60 at the Polar Bear Square, and 400 using the entire Village Green

Banquet: up to 5,000 on the Waterfowl Lake Pavilion grounds, 400 on the Mansion House porch, 60 on the Polar Bear Square, and about 200 using the entire Village Green

LOCATION

The zoo is located in Druid Hill Park, eight minutes north of the Inner Harbor, and just off Exit 7 (Druid Park Lake Drive) of the Jones Falls Expressway (I-83).

FOOD/BEVERAGE

Catering is available through the zoo or you can choose your own caterer (there may be fees if you choose your own.) Only beer and wine are allowed unless you obtain a one-day special exception license from the city to serve hard liquor. The zoo has two fully equipped kitchens, one in the Mansion House and one at the Village Green location.

LIMITATIONS/RESTRICTIONS

The Waterfowl Lake Pavilion and grounds are available year-round, anytime. You may rent the Mansion House porch after 5:00 P.M. weekdays and all day Saturday and Sunday. The Village Green is available after 5:30 P.M. any day year-round. The Polar Bear Square may be reserved anytime. The entire zoo may be rented after 5:30 P.M. any day, year-round. Music outside must be kept to a reasonable volume to protect the animals.

LEAD TIME FOR RESERVATIONS

Call at least a month in advance.

RATES

Mansion House porch: $250 per hour.
Waterfowl Lake Pavilion and grounds: rates start at $250, plus group rate costs ($5.20 for adults, $2.80 for seniors and for children) and go up proportionately from there.
Rates for the rental of the individual tented areas, the entire Village Green or the entire zoo vary according to type of organization, type of event, and number of people involved. When you choose to use an outside caterer, the zoo usually charges you a small fee to cover its costs for having to make special arrangements.

FACILITIES FOR THE PHYSICALLY HANDICAPPED?
YES NO SOME
X

BLOB'S PARK

8024 Blob's Park Road
Jessup, Maryland 20794
410/799-0155

Party on down in the polka palace

If the name Blob's Park sounds familiar it's probably because you read an article about it once in the newspaper or saw a story about the place on one of those Sunday morning news magazine television shows. Maybe you've actually been to Blob's, in which case you've discovered for yourself what all the fuss is about. Blob's Park is a Bavarian biergarten and polka palace, a monument to German food, German beer (45 different brands), German music, and German gemutlichkeit (that sort of warm, fuzzy feeling of friendship that comes with having a good time).

Open to the public on Friday and Saturday nights and Sundays, the biergarten is available for private functions during the week. Here's what you get: a huge hall with paneled walls, a 2,000-square-foot dance floor, long communal tables, straight-backed, red-cushioned chairs, a bandstand, a bar, and decorative displays of fancy beer steins and whiskey decanters. You can go the German route in your menu and music or do your own thing; it's up to you.

Next to the biergarten is the outdoor pavilion, which you may rent for either a weekday or weekend event. The covered pavilion is large, has openings on four sides, a concrete floor, and exposed beams overhead.

Blob's Park is situated on 260 acres in countryside bordering the Baltimore-Washington Parkway and Route 175. The name derives from Maximilian Blob, who got the original good times going in 1933 when he built a small bowling alley/dance club for friends who had come over from the old country. Since then, the Blob family has kept the business in continuous operation, adding on to Max's structure seven times over the years to accommodate the ever greater crowds who congregate here.

CAPACITY

Reception: 900 in the biergarten, 600 in the pavilion, 1,500 using both structures
Banquet: 900 in the biergarten, 600 in the pavilion, 1,500 using both structures

LOCATION

Take the Baltimore-Washington Parkway (I-295) south to Rt. 175 east towards Odenton, Maryland. Follow Rt. 175 to Blob's Park Road and turn right. Continue 0.2 miles to the park.

FOOD/BEVERAGE

The site prefers that you use their in-house catering service, which features a German and American menu.

LIMITATIONS/RESTRICTIONS

The biergarten is available for rentals Monday through Thursday, from 10:00 A.M. to MIDNIGHT, and Friday, from 10:00 A.M. to 5:00 P.M. The pavilion and grounds are available anytime.

LEAD TIME FOR RESERVATIONS

Biergarten: call a month in advance.
Pavilion: call a year in advance.

RATES

Pavilion: $450 per day. This rate entitles you to the use of the grounds, including the baseball field, playground, basketball and volley ball courts, as well as the pavilion. There is no rental charge for the biergarten. Food costs range from $12 to $20 per person, depending on your menu and drink choices.

FACILITIES FOR THE PHYSICALLY HANDICAPPED?
YES NO SOME
   X

CAMP GLYNDON

407 Central Avenue

Reisterstown, Maryland 21136

410/486-5515

Mailing address: American Diabetes Association

2 Reservoir Circle

Suite 203

Baltimore, Maryland 21208

A playground for kids and adults

You might not want to have your wedding here—although some people do—but for company picnics and the like, Camp Glyndon serves quite well. From the middle of June through the middle of August the camp entertains throngs of diabetic children—the camp is owned by the Maryland Chapter of the American Diabetes Association. Camp Glyndon is available for public rentals on select dates during this two-month period and at any time throughout the rest of the year.

In terms of amusements, Camp Glyndon's 63 acres offer tennis and basketball courts, an Olympic-sized pool, a softball field, a playground, volleyball equipment, horseshoes, paddleboats, and fishing. You can bunk together in cabins for overnight stays and gather groups together for meetings and mixers in the multi-purpose Leonard Levine Center, the pavilion, or the dining hall. The pitched roof pavilion includes a stage and a barbeque pit; the other two structures are plain and utilitarian in appearance. For outdoor functions, the camp's fields easily accommodate 1,000 guests or more.

CAPACITY

Picnic: up to 1,500
Overnight accommodations: 15 cabins that can sleep 200 people

in the warmer months and 40 to 50 guests in the winter months
(only six of the cabins are heated)
Reception: 225 in the pavilion
Meeting/banquet: 175 in the pavilion, 125 in the dining hall,
and about 100 in the Leonard Levine Building

LOCATION

From the Baltimore Beltway (I-695), take I-795 north, to
Reisterstown Road. Follow Reisterstown Road north, which
becomes Butler Road. From Butler Road, turn right on Central
Avenue. Proceed .9 of a mile to Insulin Lane, where you turn
left into the camp.

FOOD/BEVERAGE

The camp usually works with two local caterers but will
consider others. There is a large kitchen in the dining hall.

LIMITATIONS/RESTRICTIONS

The camp is unavailable to outside groups whenever the children
are here. The camp allows only one event to take place at a
time. Smoking is prohibited in the cabins.

LEAD TIME FOR RESERVATIONS

The camp starts booking events on January 2 for the coming
year and recommends that you call then to reserve your date.

RATES

The rate for picnics is $7 per person up to 200 people, and $6
per person for each additional person above 200, with a
minimum of 100 people required to reserve the camp. This fee
allows you full use of the camp's facilities, barring the overnight
cabins. Cabins are $75 each. The dining hall, Leonard Levine
Center, and pavilion are $150 each.

FACILITIES FOR THE PHYSICALLY HANDICAPPED?
YES NO SOME
X

DANIELLE'S BLUECREST

401 Reisterstown Road
Baltimore, Maryland 21208
410/486-2100
FAX: 410/486-1682

Two ballrooms on Pikesville's main drag

Some might say that throwing a party at Danielle's is no different from having one at a hotel, and to a certain extent they're right. The Grand Ballroom has the feel of a hotel banquet hall, with its huge dance floor and surrounding floral green carpet, massive cone-shaped chandeliers, good-sized stage, and panels of mirrors in fabric-covered side walls. The Orchid Room is a smaller, plainer spot, with a parquet floor, white walls and woodwork. As is usually true in a hotel, you can decorate these rooms to your heart's content.

What distinguishes Danielle's from a hotel are three things: First of all, the building is for your use only; Danielle's is the headquarters of a longtime Baltimore catering firm specializing in kosher menus; and you are welcome to provide your own liquor. If these unique qualities appeal, start planning now, for Danielle's is popular year-round.

CAPACITY
Reception: 1,500 using both rooms, 850 in the Grand, 350 in the Orchid
Banquet: 750 using both rooms (note: the rooms don't connect), 500 in the Grand, 165 in the Orchid

LOCATION
From the Baltimore Beltway (I-695), take the Pikesville exit and head in the direction of Baltimore. Follow Reisterstown Road south about two miles to the Bluecrest building on the left.

FOOD/BEVERAGE

The catering firm handles all your catering needs—allowing you to take care of the liquor arrangements, if you desire. Although kosher food is the specialty here, the caterer can prepare an international repertoire of menus. The catering kitchen is right off the Grand Ballroom.

LIMITATIONS/RESTRICTIONS

None.

LEAD TIME FOR RESERVATIONS

Call for availability.

RATES

There are catering fees, but no rental charges. Lunches start at $18 per person, and dinners start at $22 per person.

FACILITIES FOR THE PHYSICALLY HANDICAPPED?
YES NO SOME
X

MARYLAND SCIENCE CENTER

601 Light Street (Key Highway at the Inner Harbor)
Baltimore, Maryland 21230
410/685-2370

Where science and scenery set the pace

"Other sites on the water say they have a great view of the harbor, but they're all facing us," notes the special events manager for the Maryland Science Center. The great brick and glass-fronted complex sprawls on the other side of the inlet from Harborplace and the downtown area, giving you an unobstructed view of the harbor, the waterfront and boats, and a slice of the Baltimore skyline.

You may rent the whole museum or just a portion of it. The rooftop terrace and the center's highest floor (the third) provide the best overlooks on the scenery. When you tire of gazing outward, turn your attention to the interior attractions. The center invites you and your guests to explore its hands-on facility, top to bottom. Here you may test your knowledge of the principles of energy, learn the secrets behind the making of movies, teach yourself how to build a structure in either the Gothic, Roman, or Greek architectural style, or take a crash course on the history and life of the Chesapeake Bay. (Exhibits change sporadically, but this list gives you an idea of the kinds of activities the center offers.)

Adjoining the center are the Davis Planetarium and the cylindrically shaped IMAX Theater featuring a five-story-high movie screen. The Planetarium is available for viewing during your event; the theater may be used for business meetings, slide presentations, and IMAX films.

CAPACITY
Science Center—reception: from 20 to 1,200; banquet: from 20 to 400. The numbers vary depending upon the amount of space

233

taken up by exhibits and the location of your event within the center.
Rooftop terrace—reception: 300; banquet: 200
IMAX Theater: 400
Planetarium: 150

LOCATION

At the junction of Key Highway and Light Street on the Inner Harbor.

FOOD/BEVERAGE

You choose your own caterer. There is no kitchen here, so caterers must set up their equipment within designated "staging areas."

LIMITATIONS/RESTRICTIONS

The center is available only to corporate and nonprofit organizations, who may use the site during the summer on Monday through Thursday, from 6:00 P.M. to 11:00 P.M., and Friday through Sunday, from 9:00 P.M. to MIDNIGHT; and the rest of the year on Monday through Friday, from 6:00 P.M. to 11:00 P.M., and weekends subject to the center's own schedule of events. Smoking is not permitted anywhere in the center.

LEAD TIME FOR RESERVATIONS

Call at least three months in advance.

RATES

Science Center: rates start at $2,000 for use of the whole museum. You should call for more exact rate information, including how much it costs to rent individual areas of the museum.
Rooftop terrace: a flat fee of $750.
IMAX Theater: rates start at $1,000.
Davis Planetarium: $250 per show for an audience of 150 people.

FACILITIES FOR THE PHYSICALLY HANDICAPPED?
YES NO SOME
X

NATIONAL AQUARIUM IN BALTIMORE

501 East Pratt Street, at Pier 3
Baltimore, Maryland 21202
410/576-8740

Have a whale of a time at this water world!

Wander a while in this magical water kingdom and you'll witness bizarre-looking stingrays flapping around in an open pool, flashlight fish and electric eels glowing in the dark, puffins—those cute water birds native to the sea cliffs of the north Atlantic—peering back at you through the glass, sharks, piranhas, bottlenose dolphins, beluga whales, and nearly 5,000 other sea creatures and amphibians living within this two-million-gallons-of-water habitat.

The main building's design sets off the exhibits most dramatically and, as it happens, works rather effectively for party settings, as well. There are four rentable levels, but the space is open and contiguous, with ramps and moving walkways taking you gradually upward, so you never get a sense of being apart from the goings-on. Levels one, three, and four of the structure include areas where you can set up food and bar service. In addition, the fourth floor holds the Knott Harbor View Room, a banquet hall with a glass wall looking out on the harbor and the opposite wall covered with a blown-up photograph of the harbor taken at the turn of the century. The aquarium also offers the Lyn P. Meyerhoff Auditorium for use on the first floor.

And then there's the newly opened Marine Mammal Pavilion, connected by an inside bridge to the main building. The pavilion's Lyn P. Meyerhoff Amphitheater has seats for 1,300 spectators of its performing dolphins and whales. Elsewhere in the two-level pavilion are an arcade of hands-on exhibits and a large atrium area. The cement terrace, Pier 3, behind the main building, is also available for functions, with or without the rental of the aquarium structures. For large parties (3,000 or so guests), you can use both aquarium structures and the pier. For really big shows, the aquarium can direct you to rental boats available, which you can use in tandem with the aquarium's facilities to supplement your space.

CAPACITY

Reception: up to 3,500 people using all available space including the aquarium's main building, the Marine Mammal Pavilion, and Pier 3. If you rent two large boats, you can up the number to 5,000. Otherwise, the aquarium's main building holds 1,000, its Knott Harbor View Room holds 150, and its Marine Mammal Pavilion 1,500.
Banquet: 400 in the Marine Mammal Pavilion, 500 on the pier, and 100 in the Knott Harbor View Room
Performance/lecture: 275 in the Lyn P. Meyerhoff Auditorium.

LOCATION

On Pier 3 at the Inner Harbor.

FOOD/BEVERAGE

The aquarium has a list of 20 or so preferred caterers, from which you must choose. There is a fully equipped kitchen in each of the aquarium's buildings.

LIMITATIONS/RESTRICTIONS

The two buildings are available from mid-September through mid-May every day except Friday, and mid-May through mid-September, Monday through Thursday only. The main aquarium building may be used from 7:30 P.M. to 11:00 P.M. and the Marine Mammal Pavilion may be used from 7:30 P.M. to 10:00 P.M. The Knott Harbor View Room is available year-round from 8:00 A.M. to 4:00 P.M., Fridays from 8:00 A.M. until 9:30 P.M., and Saturdays and Sundays, mid-May through mid-September from 8:00 A.M. to 9:30 P.M. The back terrace of Pier 3 is available year-round, from 8:00 A.M. to MIDNIGHT. Smoking is allowed on the pier and in the Knott Harbor View Room only. Dancing and amplified music are permitted on the pier but not in the buildings (you can have soft music inside). Sit-down functions are confined to the Knott Harbor View Room and the Marine Mammal Pavilion Atrium.

LEAD TIME FOR RESERVATIONS

Call for availability.

RATES

Knott Harbor View Room: $1,000 for three hours, plus $200 for each additional hour. A tour of the aquarium is included. Aquarium, main building: a base fee of $1,800. Depending upon the day of the week, time of the year, time of your party, and number of people in your party, you may be charged an additional $8 per person cost for each person over a specified limit. Marine Mammal Pavilion: $3,000 for the first 300 people and $6 for each additional person.
Pier 3: $1,000 for three hours' use, plus $200 for each additional hour. Passes to tour the aquarium are obtainable during the aquarium's regular hours, subject to availability.

FACILITIES FOR THE PHYSICALLY HANDICAPPED?
YES NO SOME
X

OREGON RIDGE LODGE AND PARK

13401 Beaver Dam Road
Cockeysville, Maryland 21030
410/887-1818
Call Monday through Friday,
between 9:00 A.M. and 2:00 P.M.

Picnic in the park or let loose in the lodge

You have your choice here. You can celebrate out of doors amidst the park's 1,000-plus wooded acres or take your party inside. Either way it's a pretty rustic setting.

The Oregon Ridge Lodge has three rooms: the Sequoia, the Shawan, and the Seneca. The Sequoia is a long hall with ceiling fans hanging from a high wood-beamed ceiling, a big brick wall hearth, windows along both walls, and a stage area. The Shawan is a standard meeting room, small with carpeting and fake paneled walls. The Seneca is a larger area and features blue carpeting, a flat wood ceiling, a view of the park, and ceiling fans.

Outside you can reserve the Westinghouse Pavilion, a wooden structure with a cement floor. When you rent the pavilion you also get the use of volleyball areas, playgrounds, and picnic tables. Other outdoor spots include a tent right behind the lodge, three picnic groves of varying sizes, or the whole park. You can arrange to use the swimming lake while you're here, too, which is a short walk through the woods from the groves. A tennis court is also available. Winter activities include sledding and cross-country skiing.

CAPACITY

Reception: 600 using the the whole lodge, 350 in the Sequoia Room, 150 in the Seneca Room

238

Banquet: 100 in the Seneca, 256 in the Sequoia, 356 using both rooms
Meeting: 25 in the Shawan Room
Tented function: up to 200
Westinghouse Pavilion: up to 125
Picnic grounds: thousands

LOCATION

From the Baltimore Beltway (I-695), take I-83 north towards York. Exit at 20B, Shawan Road West, and travel on West Shawan Road about one mile to the light at Beaver Dam Road. Make a left. Bear left after your turn to get to the park on the right-hand side.

FOOD/BEVERAGE

You may choose your own caterer. There is a preparation kitchen in the lodge.

LIMITATIONS/RESTRICTIONS

The lodge is available every day, any time of the day, with a midnight curfew. The grounds are available from 7:00 A.M. until dark, year-round. Smoking is permitted in the lodge.

LEAD TIME FOR RESERVATIONS

Lodge space: Call one year ahead for weekend functions, six months ahead for weekday use.
Outside areas: Call in January to reserve for the coming year.

RATES

Weekend events: $600 for the Sequoia, $400 for the Seneca, and $100 for the Shawan.
Weekday events: $400 for the Sequoia, $300 for the Seneca, and $50 for the Shawan.
Call for rates for outside areas.

FACILITIES FOR THE PHYSICALLY HANDICAPPED?
YES NO SOME
X

THE WALTERS ART GALLERY

600 North Charles Street
Baltimore, Maryland 21201
410/547-9000, ext. 313

Awesome settings and art wondrous to behold

If you're looking for an event site that will just blow your guests away, consider the Walters. Here, you can wallow in art: the collection of some 30,000 works includes Egyptian mummies and Greek sculpture, jewelry, tapestries, and porcelains, Old Master paintings, Impressionist master-pieces, and Asian antiquities. If the art doesn't prove too overwhelming, your guests can contemplate the fine lines of the gallery, as well: the Italian Renaissance, Revival-style designs of the original 1904 building, the castle-like stone-vaulted area used to display arms and armor, or the splen-did 1850 Hackerman House.

You can rent a portion of the museum for as little as $750 or the entire, nearly block-long gallery for $13,000. (To have access to the whole museum, you must be a corporation or nonprofit group, an institution or bonafide chartered or-ganization.) Specific areas of the Walters include the follow-ing spaces: the Arms and Armor Gallery, off the Centre Street entrance; the Renaissance Sculpture Court, all arches and columns on the outskirts of a marble-floored court, topped with a skylight ceiling and with an arcaded loggia parading around its second level; the Victorian-furnished parlor of the original Walters home; the earth-toned audi-torium; and the Pavilion Cafe by the Hackerman House, a two-story affair with white columns setting it off, and a double stairway descending to it. Individuals are welcome to use the Pavilion, but no other space.

CAPACITY

Reception: up to 3,000 throughout the entire gallery
Banquet: up to 475 using specified areas of the museum: 50 in
the Armor Gallery, 200 in the Renaissance Sculpture Court,
175 in the Pavilion, and 50 in the parlor of the original house.
Lecture/performance: 491 in the auditorium

LOCATION

The museum is situated 13 blocks north of the Inner Harbor, at
the foot of the Washington Monument in Mount Vernon Place.

FOOD/BEVERAGE

The museum can offer you a long list of approved caterers, from which you must choose. There is a small kitchen; most caterers prefer to work off the museum's loading dock.

LIMITATIONS/RESTRICTIONS

The museum is available for special events year-round, on Tuesday through Sunday, from 5:00 P.M. to MIDNIGHT, and on Mondays by request. The auditorium is available for daytime functions upon request. As mentioned above, individuals may rent only the Pavilion Cafe. Smoking is prohibited in the museum, and red wine and other red beverages are restricted. Food and drink are permitted only within designated areas.

LEAD TIME FOR RESERVATIONS

Call as soon as you have a date in mind.

RATES

Rates range from $750 for rental of the Pavilion Monday through Thursday evenings from 6:30 to 9:30 to $13,000 for use of the entire museum. Call for more exact information.

FACILITIES FOR THE PHYSICALLY HANDICAPPED?
YES NO SOME
X

Alphabetic Index

An (H) indicates sites with facilities for the handicapped.

Geographic Index

Towson

West Baltimore

Westminster and Vicinity

Topical Cross Reference

Estates

Grand Ballrooms

Great Halls

Historic Sites

Inns

Museums

Overnight Conference Centers

Parks and Pavilions

Rustic Outbuildings

School-affiliated Sites

Waterfront Locations

About the Author

Elise Hartman Ford is a native of Baltimore, Maryland. She received her B.A. in English from Holy Cross College in Worcester, Massachusetts, and worked for several years as an in-house writer for such companies as MCI, in Washington, D.C., and TRW, in Redondo Beach, California. In 1985, Ford turned full time to freelance writing for magazines, newspapers and company in-house publications. She resides in Chevy Chase, Maryland, with her husband, Jim, and their daughters, Caitlin and Lucy. UNIQUE MEETING PLACES IN GREATER BALTIMORE is the second in her series.